IDRIS
ELBA

For Felix and Harry

IDRIS ELBA

So, Now What?

THE BIOGRAPHY

JOHN BLAKE

Published by John Blake Publishing Ltd,
3 Bramber Court, 2 Bramber Road,
London W14 9PB, England

www.johnblakebooks.com

www.facebook.com/johnblakebooks f
twitter.com/jblakebooks t

First published in hardback in 2014
This edition published in 2016

ISBN: 978 1 78606 118 8

British Library Cataloguing-in-Publication Data:

A catalogue record for this book is available from the British Library.

Design by www.envydesign.co.uk

Printed in Great Britain by CPI Group (UK) Ltd

1 3 5 7 9 10 8 6 4 2

Papers used by John Blake Publishing are natural, recyclable products made from
wood grown in sustainable forests. The manufacturing processes conform to the
environmental regulations of the country of origin.

Every attempt has been made to contact the relevant copyright-holders, but some were
unobtainable. We would be grateful if the appropriate people could contact us.

CONTENTS

ACKNOWLEDGEMENTS

Love and thanks to the brightest and best boys I know: Dan, Harry and Felix. And huge thanks must go to the lovely people who picked them up, took them out and kept them entertained while this was written. You know who you are, and I really couldn't have done it without you.

PROLOGUE

As the heavy prison door swung shut with a juddering thud, and the impenetrable steel bars were locked for the night, Idris Elba knew there was no escape. The award-winning actor was incarcerated in a tiny cell in the bowels of Robben Island, and as he lay down on a narrow two-centimetre-thick mat, which was to be his bed for the night, he had no choice but to contemplate the true nature of the grave challenge that lay ahead of him. Idris was about to take on the iconic role of Nelson Mandela, one of the most inspirational and controversial figures in modern world history. The pressure weighing down on his shoulders was immense. And, in a bid to understand more about the hardship suffered by the late South African leader, he had volunteered to spend the night in the remote jail where Mandela himself was imprisoned for almost two decades.

Oscar winning Hollywood stars including Morgan Freeman and Denzel Washington had turned down the role, fearing the weight of expectation on them would be too great, uncertain that they could do justice to Mandela, a hero to millions. But Idris

Elba, a young British rising star mostly known for his TV work, had bravely agreed to tackle the role after months of anguished contemplation. He is famous for always bringing great passion to his roles, and for immersing himself totally in the character so it was no great surprise that he wanted to attempt to comprehend the depth of suffering Mandela endured. Idris begged the authorities that now run the notorious former prison to allow him to spend a long and eerily silent night in a cramped and uncomfortable cell, in the hope he might begin to glimpse the same horrors.

Nelson Mandela spent 27 years in captivity, 18 of them at Robben Island, and at first Elba's highly unorthodox request was flatly denied. The prison is now a museum and no one has spent a night there since the 1980s. But Idris was determined to relive Mandela's experience as best he could, and so he doggedly persisted, begging and pleading with the authorities in charge of the now defunct prison to allow him just one night there. Eventually, they relented and he was led down into a tiny 8ft x 7ft cell.

'They took me to one of the punishment cells,' he recalled. 'It was exactly the same dimensions as Mandela's cell with a concrete floor and a bucket in the corner. Spending the night in there gave me a little taste of what it was like to be locked up in Robben Island for all those years.'

Idris knew the experience would be an interesting one, but he was not fully prepared for the extreme level of discomfort: 'It was awful,' he said. 'It was hard to sit in; it was uncomfortable, cold, haunted and damp. Mandela did 18 years there. I only did one night.

'You could imagine the toll it must have taken on him. I think it prepared him for the rest of his journey.'

However, since Elba was not a real prisoner, for insurance

purposes he had to be issued with a mobile phone in case of an emergency. 'It was no fun,' he explained. 'They locked me in at about 7.15pm, picked me up at 7.30 the next morning. It's funny, because of insurance they insisted that I take a phone in case I needed to get out.

'They said, "If you need to, just call. The security guard is about a quarter of a mile away and he will come and open the gates." It sounds obvious to say, but there's no getting out. So the guy locked the door, asks, "You're sure you want me to leave?" and I watched him walk away.

'He locked a second door, a third door, and then a fourth. And then he was gone and it was eerily quiet. There was a single light bulb on in the cell but outside in the walkways it was very dark. It dawned on me that I wasn't getting out any time soon. And then I glanced at my phone and there was no signal!

'Freedom only becomes sacred when you lose it.'

Idris Elba has become notorious for playing tough guys on screen, but even he admitted he was seriously spooked by some rather strange noises he heard during his long and lonely night in the empty prison.

At first the silence was deafening, but in the early hours of his incarceration he gradually became convinced the spirits of previous prisoners who had occupied the cells years before had returned to haunt him: 'It was really unsettling and I swear that place is haunted,' he added. 'It's dead quiet – quieter than you can imagine – and every so often I'd hear a clang or something knocking against the bars down the corridor. And there was no one else there but me. The place is haunted.

'At one point I started to nod off, and this freezing breeze passed my face – it was the end of summer, not cold out at all – and it woke me up, the hairs on the back of my neck standing up. I guarantee you it was a spirit.

'I was hearing bangs and squeaks of gates all night – the spirits of people who were tortured and beaten and punished. The guards would live on the island, so they'd come in at four in the morning, find a guy and rape him, beat him. It was lawless. And the spirit of that is all over the place.

'I was woken by a shaft of really cold air and I thought, "Someone is coming in." I thought it was coming from the window but it was tiny. At the same time this really big flock of seagulls started flying right above the cell.

'It was a weird experience. It helped me understand a little of the mindset of a man who was incarcerated for so long.'

And once Idris had relived the experience of a man who forgave his jailers and went on to become the first black President of South Africa, changing the course of history, he felt ready to take on the role that would catapult him to superstar status and change his life forever.

CHAPTER ONE

FROM HOLLY STREET TO HOLLYWOOD

Beating well-established A-list Hollywood stars to critically acclaimed roles is now something Idris Elba coolly takes in his stride, but, having grown up on a tough and rundown housing estate in East London, he leads a luxurious lifestyle he would never have even dared to dream existed.

Born Idrissa Akuna Elba in the early hours of Wednesday, 6 September 1972, weighing in at over 10 pounds, he was to be the only child of African immigrants. And, as dawn broke that late-summer morning, his future looked decidedly bleak. His mother Eve and father Winston had arrived in London a couple of years earlier, penniless and desperate to escape a life of poverty and hardship in West Africa. After leaving Sierra Leone, Winston was delighted to land himself a steady job at the Ford car production factory in Dagenham. He vowed to work hard and never rock the boat, for fear he might end up with nothing again. Having experienced extreme poverty, his dearest wish was that his son would follow in his footsteps and lead an equally quiet and content life, with a steady salary and no more uncertainty. His young wife Eve, a typist who came to the UK from Ghana shortly after marrying Winston, also wanted nothing more than simplicity and happiness for her son.

As he grew up, Idris was made sharply aware of the misery his family had suffered before they arrived in Britain. Money was tight, and nothing was taken for granted. As a black child growing up on the troubled streets of East London, where the National Front was rapidly gaining power, he was warned repeatedly to do his best to keep out of trouble.

Now kids growing up in Hackney dream of being Idris Elba, but back then he was just like all the other boys on the Holly Street housing estate whose heroes would no doubt have included The Bionic Man, footballers George Best and John Barnes, and the actor Robert De Niro. But most of all, young Idris was fascinated by tales of his paternal grandfather Moses who proved a lifelong inspiration: 'He was a great man,' Idris recalled later. 'He raised my dad and my dad's family. I would still like to be like my own granddad.'

Idris loved to hear tales of Moses Elba, who had been a sailor and a policeman. When he was not too exhausted from long shifts at the factory, Winston would often entertain his young son with colourful tales of fearless Moses' exotic travels. Although Idris never actually met Moses, in his head his grandfather became larger than life and, as soon as he was old enough, he even had Moses Elba's name tattooed on his arm. And it was those tales of travel and adventure that led Idris to believe that he too could set out and conquer the wider world beyond his window. He just needed to find a way out of Holly Street.

While he dreamt of following in the footsteps of his grandfather's great escapades, Idris found his mother's overly protective nature could become a little smothering at times, especially when she enrolled him at Stormont House, a primary school for children with special needs, although his only health issue was asthma!

'That was a weird two years of my life,' he said, looking back on his childhood. 'Very weird. I was asthmatic but I was fine as long as I wasn't running around.

'And here I was at this amazing school that was full of kids with very severe disabilities and kids who were just straight up bad – and I was chucked in the middle of that.'

Idris may look fit and strong these days, but he still carries an inhaler and when he is in LA the pollution can be a problem: 'Smog is a big factor,' he says. 'I have to use my inhaler a lot.'

In November 2013, he also suffered a severe asthma attack on a plane prior to the South African premiere of *Mandela: Long Walk to Freedom*, which saw him briefly hospitalised.

Aside from the occasional asthma scare, life in the East End was pretty happy for Idris, especially when he left Stormont in 1977 and moved on to nearby Queensbridge Primary School: 'What I remember is the summertime,' he recalled fondly. 'Hackney was a warm, carefree place.'

Idris has idyllic memories of playing football in the streets while his dad hustled at pool in the Middleton Arms, a pub near London Fields long since demolished and replaced by an apartment block. He said: 'I'd run across the road to get some crisps – and because they loved my dad, they loved me.' He would come back laden with enough for the whole team.

'It was the best time of my life,' he continued. 'Hackney is very dear to me, it was where I learned to ride my bike and London Fields was my park of choice. I used to ride my bike around Haggerston, down the ramps and along the canal – that's what all the kids did.

'It's always good to come home whenever I'm in London.

When I'm filming, I quite often jump in the car and drive around Dalston, which is my old stomping ground. It's absolutely no surprise to me that the area is now one of the trendiest places in London – Hackney has always been cool,' he added.

In the evenings, Idris would race home for dinner in front of the television, glued to American shows such as *Dallas* and *Starsky & Hutch*, struggling to imagine what it would be like to be part of such a glamorous world.

Without any siblings for company, he would invent characters to play with, planting the early seeds of his acting career: 'I think it comes from being an only child,' he later explained. 'When you've got two toys, you do two voices. I wouldn't want to go to bed because I would be in this imaginary world playing with my toys.'

But his father found Idris's daydreams frustrating and often they would clash over school work and even football – Idris supports Arsenal, although he admits to having gone to just two matches, while Winston preferred rival team Manchester United!

But Winston made sure Idris was surrounded by their extended family every weekend, so he did not grow too lonely, and as a result he forged close relationships with his cousins. 'It really informed how I related to other kids,' he said. 'I wanted everyone to be my mate; I wanted to have close relationships. My cousins and I were really, really close when I was a kid. They used to come round and when it was time for them to leave on Sunday night, and my uncles would come to pick them up about six because it was bedtime, I used to cry.

'The house would be so empty, and it had been all laughing and joking, playing hide-and-seek, then when they left it was just me and my mum and dad. So at school I really got close to mates and I know my mates still now. They're brothers now, y'know?'

After a short stint at Laburnum Primary School in Haggerston, which he loved, Idris moved with many of his friends up to the co-educational Kingsland High School in Hackney at the age of 11. But in 1983, just two months after starting the first term, the Elba family left their ninth-floor council flat in Hackney and stepped onto the property ladder with a four-bedroom house on Braemar Street in Canning Town. Winston and Eve could not have been more proud as the house was a symbol of the great financial and social progress they had made since arriving in Britain, but Idris hated the idea of leaving his friends.

Now the street is run down, with rusty cars sitting on bricks and sofas rotting outside derelict terraced houses. Today one in five people living on the street claim income support, and, according to official figures, the same number suffer from serious long-term illness. Half of those of working age have no formal qualifications. Even the council admits that Braemar Street is in one of the top 5 per cent 'most deprived areas' in the UK.

Crime is rampant. A few years ago, parcel firm DHL added the neighbourhood to a list of 'no-go' places it deemed too dangerous to deliver to – alongside Iraq, Afghanistan and parts of Cambodia.

But for Winston, buying the property back then was a badge of honour. Little more than a decade he had left Africa virtually penniless, this was a tangible sign that he had made a success of his new life. His hard graft at the Ford factory had paid off at last.

'They were lovely people, and perfect neighbours who – unlike some these days – kept the place tidy,' recalled Audrey

O'Shea, who lived next door, and whose sons would play football in the street with Idris. 'All that Winston and Eve wanted was to have a nice life, give their son a good upbringing and be good citizens. You got the impression that's what got them up in the morning. Idris repaid them by turning into a fantastic, hard-working boy.'

But for Idris, swapping multi-racial Hackney for an area that was then mostly white and completely alien proved a traumatic change: 'I was really devastated when we left and moved to Canning Town,' he admitted.

Worse still, arriving at his new school with his mother on the first day, and observing a dining room full of boys, he noticed a glaring omission on the curriculum. 'I said to my mum, "Where do the girls eat?"' he recalled. 'The receptionist started laughing. She said, "This is a boys' school." I felt robbed

'I couldn't even understand the concept. A boys' school, what is that? Did I do something wrong? Am I in trouble?'

Already tall for his age, Elba immediately struggled to fit in with the other boys at Trinity Comprehensive School. 'I got immediately sized up,' he reflects. '"Oh yeah, we know who you are. You from Hackney, yeah? Big man." The best fighter in my year, big fucker, immediately wants to fight me.

'I can remember the sights and the smells of that school, thinking, "What am I doing here?" I'm quite an open person, and being tall and big, you find yourself alienated a little bit because you're bigger than everyone else. So I found myself talking with a softer voice and doing whatever anyone suggested at school because I wanted to fit in.'

But almost from day one Idris was a target for bullies, because of his size and race, which made him stand out from the others. He did everything he could to fit in at Trinity, without much success. The first thing he did was to shorten his name, which was of Krio African origin, because he was bullied for it sounding 'girly'. He was taunted about being called Idrissa (his full name), which led the boys to call him 'Melissa'. 'Idrissa is my name,' he said. 'Idrissa is sort of like a firstborn son, but I took off the "a" at the end because it used to get me in trouble at school. It was very feminine sounding. I'd get teased and end up beating someone up.

'As a kid, yeah, it happened often. I was really conscious that my name was so different. Everyone was called Jason or Terry or James or Michael. Then there'd be Idris. My name would always get a snicker or two when I was a little kid.' But he refused to sit idly by and allow his classmates to mock him. In fact, he did not let anyone get away with bullying: 'I quickly got well known because I was tall and I wasn't taking any shit,' he said.

From an early age Idris learned that he would have to fight for what he wanted. And what he wanted more than anything was to get out of Canning Town.

'I was born in Forest Gate and lived in Hackney and in Canning Town,' he explained. 'We moved to Canning Town when I was going into the first year of high school. That was a culture shock, on many levels. Everyone's like, "What are you doing here, you black bastard?"

'According to my parents it was nicer, but it was just as poor. It was mainly white and Indian, as opposed to Hackney, which is very mixed. Canning Town was like a slap in the face, like, "Wake up! This is the rest of the world". I was very much a Hackney lad.'

Idris has always remained loyal to his Hackney roots, and was honoured more than three decades after leaving the area when a housing project was named after him. In January 2011, he returned to his childhood home to open two new blocks of apartments, which had been named in recognition of his acting and charitable achievements.

'I was really moved,' he said after hearing about the honour. 'You can give me all the parts in the world, but that means so much. I've lived all over the place, but the only place I recognise as where I come from is Hackney.

'It is well documented that I was in Hackney for quite a long length of time. But just to have someone say: "We are so proud of what you have done we are going to name a building after you that is cost-effective, clean and new" is a great honour.

'Everyone has the right to own a home so I think this is a really good idea. I told my dad and I think he believed it less than me.'

His father Winston toured the £6.2 million housing project with his son, and when a plaque was unveiled he joked: 'I thought the building belonged to him.'

Danny Lynch, London development director for A2Dominion New Homes, said at the time: 'We're delighted to name Elba House after Idris Elba, who has strong links to the Hackney area. The block is providing much-needed high-quality new homes for affordable rent, whilst a smaller block at the scheme offers affordable homes for part-buy part-rent to help local people onto the property ladder.'

But years earlier, in the early 1980s, Idris's small, tight-knit family had struggled hard to get on the housing ladder themselves. Their decision to pack up and leave their flat in Hackney was a tough one but the traumatic move would give Idris the impetus he needed to turn his life around. From the moment he arrived in Canning Town, he became determined not to stop until he had swapped Holly Street for Hollywood.

CHAPTER TWO

STANDING OUT FROM THE CROWD

The streets of East London were tough places for black kids to find themselves in the 1980s, and, when the Elba family moved from a council flat in Hackney to a small house in Canning Town, Idris quickly realised that he stood a long way out from the crowd.

He sensed a very different atmosphere in Canning Town, which was at that time quickly becoming one of the strongholds of the far right National Front party. Without realising the full extent of the unrest, his parents had unwittingly decided to settle in an area where a political move towards unity on the far right had been steadily growing during the 1960s.

Shortly before Idris was born, the right-wing extremists got the impetus they needed when a moderate Conservative Party was defeated in the 1966 General Election. Leader of the League of Empire Loyalists A.K. Chesterton, cousin of the novelist G.K. Chesterton, argued that a racialist right-wing party would have won the election and started to gather followers at grassroots level. He opened talks with the British

National Party, led by John Tyndall, and they agreed a merger, along with the Racial Preservation Society, and so the National Front was founded on 7 February 1967.

The purpose of the National Front was to oppose immigration policies in Britain, and multinational agreements such as the United Nations or NATO as replacements for negotiated bilateral agreements between nations.

The newly formed political party, which horrified many in Britain, banned neo-Nazi groups from being allowed to join the party, but members of Tyndall's Greater Britain Movement were allowed to join and the National Front quickly swelled its ranks.

By the time Idris was starting primary school in the mid-1970s, the National Front had almost 20,000 members and 50 local branches, consisting mainly of blue-collar workers and the self-employed, who resented immigrant competition in the labour market and for scarce housing.

Some recruits came from the Monday Club within the Conservative Party, which had been founded in reaction to Harold Macmillan's 'Wind of Change' speech. Immigrant families like the Elbas were bewildered by inflammatory speeches they heard on the streets around their new home as the National Front fought to gain power on a platform of opposition to communism and liberalism, support for Ulster loyalism, opposition to the European Economic Community, and the compulsory repatriation of new Commonwealth immigrants who had entered Britain under the British Nationality Act, 1948.

But street demonstrations by the National Front were already becoming a common sight, particularly in East London, where they often faced anti-fascist protestors from opposing left-wing groups, including the International Marxist Group and the International Socialists (later the Socialist Workers Party).

The party's office manager John O'Brien, a former Conservative and supporter of Enoch Powell, replaced Chesterton in 1970, following a vote of no confidence. And then between 1973 and 1976 the National Front performed better in local elections, as well as in several parliamentary by-elections, although no parliamentary candidates ever won a seat. But there were shocks in store as their popularity surged. By 1974, the ITV documentary *This Week* had exposed the neo-Nazi pasts of several key members and tensions were running high, although the party remained popular in the East End of London, Dagenham and Canning Town.

'There was a lot of tension,' recalled Idris. 'People would pick fights with me; call me names. I used to get into fights all the time. My mentality was always, "Why not me?" At secondary school I wasn't equal because I was black.

'Canning Town was the centre of the National Front. They're an extreme right-wing party. Their beliefs are: Keep Britain White. Well, Canning Town was a hub for the National Front. So, when I got there, I realised that there was that tension there.

'Canning Town wasn't fun at that point because it was a big National Front area. It was tough and you had to stand up for yourself.'

A National Front march through central London on 15 June 1974 led to a 21-year-old man, Kevin Gately, being killed and dozens more – including 39 police officers – being injured, in violent clashes between the party's supporters and members of 'anti-fascist' organisations. In March 1975, 400 NF supporters demonstrated across London in protest against EEC membership. In the Greater London Council election of May 1977, 119,060 votes were cast in favour of the National Front and the Liberals were beaten in 33 out of 92 constituencies. Three months later, members marched through the largely non-white areas of South-East London under an inflammatory slogan claiming that 85 per cent of muggers were black while 85 per cent of their victims were white. Vicious riots broke out. Two hundred and seventy policemen and over two hundred marchers were injured, while an attempt was made by rioters to destroy the local police station.

At the riot, which is often referred to as the Battle of Lewisham, many of those who took part were not members of any 'anti-fascist' or 'anti-racist' group, but local disgruntled youths, both black and white.

The party began to fragment in 1979, and rapidly declined in the 1980s, leading to the formation of the British National Party, but emotions continued to run high, racist abuse was commonplace and it was a frightening time for black families living on predominantly white housing estates.

'I wasn't going to be a part of that at all,' said Idris. 'I'm from Hackney. I used to get in fights with white kids all the time because they were stamping all over people. I was like, "Fuck that".

'They were picking fights with me. Walking down the street someone would call you a black c**t. "What? Who the fuck you talking to?" Then Mum says, "No, no, no, leave it, leave it! It's all right, leave it." "No! What? It ain't all right. Who you talking to?" Fight.

'I got quickly well known in my neighbourhood because I was a tall guy but I just wasn't taking any shit.'

While his mother pleaded with Idris not to take the bait, and to stay away from fist-fights, his father disagreed and taught him to stand up to the racist bullies.

'The school I was at had a lot of black and Asian kids and a few white kids,' Elba remembered. 'We came out of school and sure enough, there would be lads waiting for you, picking on people. It never got much worse than that but I had to defend myself a few times.

'My old man was very much, "Fight fire with fire". If I came home and said, "Oh, I'm being picked on," he just told me to go out there and sort it out.'

But having to deal with a steady stream of abuse at school and in the streets around his home proved upsetting for Idris. He found himself one of very few black faces in a sea of white boys who took against him with a vengeance at Trinity Comprehensive School: 'My school was all boys, aggressive. I'd be chased home by a bunch of white boys; I got into scuffles. It never got to the stage where I was hospitalised but it was street law and you had to deal with it,' he recalled.

'I was a dreamer. Always. I didn't see why I shouldn't have equal standing. I wondered why didn't I get to be cocky and wear the good trainers?'

Luckily, Idris, who is now 6ft 3in, shot up fast when he hit puberty and found himself able to stand up to the racists and the bullies, not just because of his tough mental attitude, but also because of his sheer physical stature. And since he was a county-level runner and excelled on the football pitch, some of the boys gradually started to respect him for that: 'Because I was big, I didn't have to listen to anyone doubting me,' he said. 'I was just considered good at football or whatever, there were no questions about it.'

Although his efforts were appreciated on the football team, throughout his school years Idris was only too sharply aware that his African heritage stood him apart from the other pupils in his predominantly white school, even though he had, in fact, been born just a few miles away.

And yet, looking back years later, he expressed a nostalgic fondness for the school, which no longer exists: 'I miss my great school there, Trinity, which was knocked down,' he said. 'I love coming back. My mum still lives in Newham and I'm always there – I never felt like I left it.'

As a teenager, it would have been very easy for Idris to fall in with the wrong crowd and he later admitted to having bought his first car illegally at the age of 14, which he drove to school without telling his parents. With a part-time job as a tyre fitter, he had managed to secretly save up enough cash to buy the car, a Mini Clubman, and drove it without any licence or insurance since he was far too young to take the driving test. Of course, Winston and Eve had no idea that the vehicle, which he hid in the garage where he worked, even existed.

'By the time I was 14 I realised I had an obsession with speed, bought myself a car and that was it, I never looked back,' he revealed. 'The Mini was a sign of my liberation – I drove it to school every day. To buy a car at 14 one must have facial hair, because, when you do at 14, people don't question your age.

'I'm not proud of my exploits but for me it's where it all began. My parents don't know I bought it!'

CHAPTER THREE

A ROYAL FAVOUR

Idris grew up fast and strong, learned to defend himself and managed to keep the bullies at bay, but it was during those turbulent teenage years that his school work began to suffer as he started to lose interest in his academic lessons: 'I wasn't bad at school,' he said. 'But I was never a bookworm.'

Luckily drama classes, and more specifically his dedicated teacher, Susan McPhee, came to his rescue. 'I'm quite a shy man,' he admitted, 'and I was a shy, shy kid. I wasn't the life of the party. But then I remember being in drama at school, being 14 or 15, and I remember Miss McPhee saying, "You're good, you're really good."'

'She was astounded by me – she was the actual influence.'

And it was only when he was taken under the wing of Miss McPhee that Idris actually began to suspect there could be a way out of Canning Town after all. She unearthed his talent for acting, and managed to convince him that he really had great potential, and that he should pursue acting as a possible career option. But it took a lot of guts for Idris, the quiet kid at a tough all-boys school, to stand up and recite passages from Shakespeare in front of the entire class.

And yet he found speaking someone else's words helped him beat the bullies: 'Even with people looking at you, when you're playing a character, you're so hidden,' he explained. 'There's a weird little thing there, where you just feel most comfortable being someone else, because then they're not really looking at you.'

After leaving school at 16, Idris agreed to continue his education, much to the delight of his parents, and in 1988 he enrolled on a two-year course to gain a BTech in performing arts at nearby Barking & Dagenham College. 'This was a great place to learn,' he said. 'Barking & Dagenham College was the first place I got to fall on my face as an actor and get back up to be supported by great people and a great college.'

'From the start, his talent was obvious,' recalls John McDermott, his former drama teacher at the college. 'Idris was a huge young man with a formidable stage presence but what really stood out was his work ethic.

'It was tough, doing nights at the car plant and days in college, but he never asked for sympathy; he didn't want to be a burden on his parents. It took a great deal of character and perseverance for him to see it through.'

Miss McPhee also gave him another much-needed confidence boost by fixing him up with a Youth Training Scheme placement at Barking Town Hall, where he learned everything from scenery shifting to ballet. He also struck up his first show business friendship – with the television presenter Danny Baker, who was working at the theatre at the time, starring as Idle Jack in the pantomime *Dick Whittington*.

While he loved what little acting he was doing, Idris was not sure in which direction to take his career. Struggling to make ends meet, he had started to earn a little extra money by dabbling in modelling after being told he had the right look, although he himself was never convinced he had what it takes to strut his stuff on the catwalk: 'At that stage, clearly I was not focused,' he said. 'As a kid I sort of blended into the background quite a bit. I wasn't the guy that was a big personality, I was the tall, silent, quiet type.

'I call it the invisible factor. On any ordinary street, walking down in London, Soho in a cap, I'm just a fucking tall black man walking along.

'I was tall. I was never going to be a professional model but it was a step in the right direction. I was in college doing a performing arts course. Two years of drama, acting, dancing, singing, directing and everything, and the modelling was sort of like doing catwalk shows in, you know, Walthamstow Town Hall, but they were good fun and I think my ambition grew.'

Idris enjoyed the training scheme and he loved participating in amateur dramatics, but it was an unfamiliar world and there were plenty of other distractions back in those early days. He was a county-level runner by that stage, and it took up so much of his time that he even considered sacrificing acting to pursue his love of athletics instead: 'When I was 15 and 16 I used to run for the Essex Beagles and I used to run a 10.12-second 100 metres,' he recalled. 'I was second in Newham. If I'd kept that up at that age I would have been an Olympic runner. No doubt. But it wasn't my thing.'

Idris was also a highly talented footballer and a rising star on the local DJ scene. He had begun helping his uncle with his wedding DJ business in 1986, and within a year started his own company with some friends. On top of that, he was also beginning to discover the effect he had on women.

And, of course, he faced immense pressure from his hardworking father to settle down with a secure job to provide for his future. But Idris wanted more, much more. 'As I got into my teens, my ambition to be the cool cat was bigger, the appetite was there,' he said. 'I discovered women loved me and I could have gone down a route that was not criminal but cutting corners. But instead I ended up in tights doing ballet at a performing arts course. I don't think anyone expected that – and I don't think anyone but me expected anything from that.

'I didn't know any actors, I just knew it was something I liked. One minute I'm playing football then I'm doing ballet in tights. But I liked it, I liked the discipline – it was different.'

Although money for extra-curricular dance and drama lessons was tight, Idris remembers his parents were always careful to nurture his creativity: 'I was an only child and, while I wasn't spoilt, I remember that they used to make me get up and sing songs to them and do break-dancing, all the stuff that was confidence building and turned me into what I am today,' he said.

Once Idris finished college, in 1990, his dedicated drama teacher Sue McPhee helped arrange a grant to enable him to take a course at the National Youth Music Theatre. And that was the moment his life changed forever. The course was expensive so Winston insisted on Idris paying his way by taking a part-time job at the Ford factory. And to help cover the fees, he and Sue applied for, and won, a £1,500 scholarship from the prestigious Prince's Trust, a charity he continues to support passionately. He is an anti-knife crime ambassador for the Prince of Wales' charity, helping kids get away from gang culture to find their talents.

'I'm a recipient of The Prince's Trust generosity – I got £1,500 to help me get into the National Youth Music Theatre, which was a lot of money back then,' he has since said. 'I probably wouldn't have gone if they hadn't given me that. That was a life-changing experience for me.

'I grew up in Hackney, one of London's most deprived boroughs. The area was crawling with gangs, crime and poverty, and the lack of role models meant that many of my friends felt they had nowhere to turn.

'It's easy to see why so many of my peers didn't do well at school and subsequently succumbed to the "easy" life – mixing with the wrong crowd and heading down the wrong path to a life of unemployment and sometimes even drugs.

'It's frightening to see that this is still happening in communities across the UK. It is these young people – those who have already resigned themselves to life on the dole – that need our help the most.

'I was lucky. I had the support of my family and teachers who nurtured my ambitions. That's not to say my early years were easy – far from it. Living in an area with high racial tension meant I often got chased home by groups of people who had singled me out for being different.

'I left school with dreams of attending the National Youth Music Theatre but was disheartened when I realised how much it would cost. It was The Prince's Trust who made it possible. They gave me a £1,500 grant and set me on the path that would eventually change my life. I have a daughter and I'd be heart-broken if she was to experience long-term unemployment or felt she had no one to turn to. There are hundreds of thousands of young people out there who are sadly in this position.

'This is why I'm such a passionate ambassador for The Prince's Trust. In my role I've been fortunate to meet with some of the young people who have been supported by the Trust. And these visits have only confirmed to me the importance of inspiring the next generation.

'Anything is possible, even if you don't quite make your grades this summer.

'With the right support – through organisations like the Trust – it is possible to achieve your dreams. I am living proof of that.'

Regardless of the wealth, fame and awards he accumulates, Elba remains resolutely proud of his East End roots to this day, and was delighted to be guest of honour at the Hackney Picture House's National Youth Film Festival in October 2013. He explained: 'Students can be bedazzled by all the lights and cameras but, when they meet someone and can actually put a face to it, it's tangible, a real person and a real career choice and I think students can get influenced by that.

'National Youth Film Festival is a great festival and it gives kids an opportunity to see lots of film and get to meet people who are in the industry. I think that kids across the nation will definitely benefit and I think there needs to be more festivals like this. So it's a good thing, thumbs up.'

He also explained why speaking directly to young people growing up in his old neighbourhood held so much personal importance for him: 'One, it was in a neighbourhood that nurtured me as a kid, Hackney, and, two, I know that it's important for people that are on the way up or working to be able to engage with kids.

'I know how important it is because it happened to me as a kid. It was great in the sense that this festival has created that forum, so I was definitely "That would be a good thing to do", and it would be positive. If they show up, I'll show up!'

Idris remains concerned about the welfare of young people growing up in his old stomping ground, which still has a reputation for violence and street crime: 'Young people find comfort in gangs and, once that happens, their lives change,' he said. 'But I think Hackney is a borough that cares for people, you go to Hackney and there is a sense of pride.

'Education is the key – stick with it and don't let your guard down; the more you know about what you want to do the better. I'd still encourage young people to keep an eye out for open auditions but it's an interesting point.

'If I was growing up now, I'd have made a film – get a couple of mates and a mobile phone and make people see your talent, tell the story of where you're from. There's a lot of opportunity if you help make it happen.

'Kids from here can achieve, they need to say, "Yo, I'm from Hackney and I'm proud". Like Jay-Z, he's from Brooklyn and he says how proud he is.

'People start to shun the bad things that other people say about a place and the whole community gets behind it.'

But Idris was not always so confident that he could really make it big in the unknown world of acting. One of the biggest problems holding him back in his teens was that none of his friends had the slightest interest in following him down a similar path, and it made him stand out from the crowd even more: 'All my other mates were DJs or drug dealers or whatever. They didn't want to know about acting,' he said.

But he decided to go for it, and soon after joining the National Youth Music Theatre he publicly sang for the first time in an acclaimed production of *Guys and Dolls*, which was so successful he was invited to join a tour of Japan.

Idris was electrified by the thrill of being on stage and adored the applause from the audience, but work was hard to come by and for a while the biggest part he could land was in a BBC *Crimewatch* drama reconstruction about a suspect who chopped up his girlfriend and put her body parts in the freezer.

'We shot it at the actual crime scene,' he said later. 'They'd stripped the walls because of the blood, so that was a nice day at the office!'

Between roles, Idris had to take whatever work he could,

trying everything from tyre fitting to cold-calling advertising sales to pay the rent to his parents. There was the occasional modelling gig, and in 1992 he also started working in nightclubs under the DJ name Big Driis, beginning a love affair with music that continues to this day. What he did not want was to follow his father into a lifelong career at a factory.

CHAPTER FOUR

CHASING CARS

Although the acting parts he was landing after college were small at first, Idris was gradually growing in confidence, despite having his thespian aspirations strongly discouraged by his anxious family. His parents Eve and Winston feared acting would not provide him with a steady income or a predictable future, and Winston insisted a job like his at the Ford car factory would lead to a far more promising career.

For a while Idris resisted as hard as he could, instead attempting to pay his way by carving out a niche for himself as a DJ. Having spent much of his childhood listening to his father's soul records, he grew up loving music and leapt at the chance to earn a little extra pocket money by helping out his uncle, who provided the music at local weddings: 'For Afro-Caribbean weddings I was playing a lot of African, calypso and reggae-type jam,' he smiled, recalling happy times. When he reached the age of 14, he had been allowed to take over basic mixing duties while his uncle was making moves on the dance floor. The first song he ever played was

'Hot Hot Hot' by Arrow, a guaranteed dance-floor filler in the early 1980s.

Soon afterwards, he and a friend, known simply as Boogie, who is still his DJ partner 25 years on, inherited a pair of turntables when their school closed its music department and sold off all the equipment. And so, by the time he turned 16, Idris and Boogie had started a sound system known as Social Affair. Not long afterwards, he landed himself a regular slot on Climax FM, a pirate radio station, calling himself Mr Kipling after the famous cake maker, because of his 'exceedingly good tunes'. However, some claim the nickname actually came about because of his rapacious reputation with women: 'It was because I was a ladies' man,' he grinned. 'The boys said to me: "Idris, you've got more tarts than Mr Kipling."' He himself rather enjoys the mystery and will only say with a wry smile: 'I've outgrown DJ names now.'

After dispensing with Mr Kipling, he adopted the moniker of Driis, a shortened version of his real name Idrissa, which he still uses for DJ gigs now. Unsurprisingly, his law-abiding parents were horrified by their son's frequent run-ins with the police, who would regularly attempt to close down his under-the-radar radio station. 'There were plenty of knocks on the door – "doof, doof, doof" and we'd be out,' he recalled. 'And in those times we had to work with vinyl and CDs so we had to lug a lot of stuff away. But we were pretty savvy lads – we'd move it around and if you got a place high enough the DTLR [the former Department for Transport Local Government and the Regions] just couldn't be bothered. "They went up where? Leave it." Any council flats, though, and they'll normally get you.'

It was hip-hop's golden age, the era of Snoop Dogg, Tupac, Biggie Smalls and Dr Dre. Determined to keep up with the trends, Idris would devour every new issue of *Vibe* magazine, for all the fashion, beats and lingo of black America. He dreamt of crossing the Atlantic and starting a new life. Good-looking and charming, but unable to make ends meet as a DJ, he found work as a wide-eyed intern at Bad Boy Records, Sean 'P. Diddy' Combs' first label.

When P. Diddy came to speak at a music seminar in Islington, North London, in the early nineties, Idris queued for three hours to get a good seat. And when he saw his idol, he admits to being utterly starstruck.

'That was when Bad Boy was like BAD BOY,' he said. 'This guy was killing the game. And when he finished his speech, he walked straight down the middle of the aisle, dapping people. I remember I put my hand out and he dapped me. I was like, "Yo! Puffy Combs dapped me!"'

He could have had no idea back then that one day he would be hanging out alongside Combs in the coolest celebrity circles, or that Combs himself would admit to being a huge fan of Elba's.

Looking back, Idris says it was his early attempts at being a DJ that gave him a much-needed confidence boost but still not quite enough to launch his career: 'When I left school I got into small, local theatre groups and at the same time I was DJing on a radio station, so the two worlds were pretty weird and odd,' he said. 'But the transition was pretty smooth. I had confidence when I was on the radio and I used that confidence to get into my first job as an actor.'

But simply having confidence was not enough. Eventually, he had no other option but to put his dreams on hold and do as his father repeatedly asked. In 1991 he went to work full time on the night shift on the factory floor of the Ford car plant in East London, welding side panels onto a never-ending procession of Ford Fiestas: 'I went to work night shifts with my dad for a year at Ford and that's when I bucked my ideas up because it was real hard work,' he said. 'And I didn't want to stay there for the rest of my life, so I had to focus.'

Although his father was delighted that his son had finally seen sense, the work was dull and repetitive, and it was not a happy time for Idris who was often in trouble with his boss because he would fall asleep as car after car passed him by, so it would move on to the next fitter with a panel missing. He has joked to this day there are people driving around in Ford Fiestas missing their bottom welds on his account!

Idris endured the job for a year, bored and hating every minute of it, but he did not dare complain to his father, who had been patiently doing this same repetitive job for 30 years without a murmur. But the crunch came one night after Idris lost patience and abandoned his station following yet another heated argument with his supervisor during a shift.

Idris recalled: 'About four or five in the morning I got back to my station and my supervisor is going, "Where the fuck have you been? Who do you think you are? You're supposed to be working! You're gonna get disciplinary action."'

But, as he roamed aimlessly round the factory floor in the early hours of that day in 1991, Idris had been doing a lot of thinking and had already decided that he definitely could not spend the rest of his life working there. Already he had a little acting experience, thanks to the National Youth Music Theatre, which gave him the confidence he needed to make the leap.

'I said to my supervisor, "Bruv, don't worry about it, I'm going. I'm gonna act. I'll see you later,"' Idris added.

That late-summer morning he walked out of the factory and went straight into a local branch of STA Travel. Using an out-of-date student card, he bought himself a discounted return ticket to New York for £179. He withdrew his last £300 from the bank, and later that night went back to the factory for the final time. Idris headed straight into his father's office to say goodbye.

It was a conversation he had dreaded, but Idris could wait no longer. By this time, Winston had risen through the ranks and had become a foreman with his own office and a number of privileges, which included the keys to a little sports buggy used to speed around the factory. In the middle of their awkward and emotionally charged farewell, Idris swiped the keys from his father's desk.

As well as a plane ticket, Idris had also treated himself to a few beers earlier that evening, to help pluck up the courage to tell his father of his plan. And so at 1am he drunkenly decided it would be a good idea to take the buggy for a joy ride around the vast factory, which is about the size of Disneyland.

'It was freezing out, just driving around that whole plant,' he recalled later. 'I had a Walkman, and I had Sam Cooke on it. That's all it was: Sam Cooke, the whole album. Sipped from that beer like, "Fuck this world".'

After a couple of hours, Idris returned to the office at 3am to find an enraged supervisor, and behind him, an equally furious father. He handed back the keys and walked out of the factory for the last time, vowing never to look back.

'The next day I was in New York for the first time,' he said. With almost no money to his name, and aged just 19, he stayed at the YMCA in Manhattan's Union Square and began scouring the newspapers for casting notices.

CHAPTER FIVE

A BITE OF THE BIG APPLE

Life in New York was not quite how Idris had imagined it. Convinced the starring role of his dreams would land in his lap, he had arrived in the Big Apple brimming with confidence but with very little cash, and certainly no back-up plan. All he knew was that he could not stay at home any longer. 'It happened at a time when I wasn't making any money from acting,' he remembers. 'I was doing a night shift at the Ford factory with my dad and I knew that if I stayed there I'd be a lifer. I took the moment to say: "Stop, go for it". The next morning I took a flight to New York. Backpack. YMCA. I didn't get a job.'

After just a week, he realised that he would have to give up on his dream of attending drama school, when he was rejected by the Lee Strasberg Theatre and Film Institute in Manhattan, and had no choice but to return home to the UK and to move back in with his parents, although he was determined not to stay there for long. His love affair with the USA had begun.

'I tried to get into the Lee Strasberg school but there was all sorts of red tape,' he explained. 'But it gave me the energy to come back and do it. When I got back to London, the first thing I did was get a play.

'My dad said, "You want to be an actor, that's fantastic, but while you live under this roof you need to pay some bills."'

Trying to do the right thing, and eager to make amends with his father, who was furious with him for walking out on a steady job, Idris pledged to settle down, to get married and find a regular job. His long-term relationship to a beautiful Liberian actress called Dormowa Sherman had fizzled out. Many press reports claim he married Dormowa and she was the mother of his child, but it later emerged that in June 1998 he tied the knot with Hanne Norgaard at Chelsea Register Office, and they later had a daughter together.

'I liked the idea of being married,' he explained. 'I was focused in on what I was trying to do in my life and my girl supported me.'

Idris hit the audition circuit and managed to land himself a few minor roles on primetime TV, including an episode of the British sitcom *2Point4 Children* in 2004, and the part of a male escort hired by Patsy and Edina in a hilarious episode of the BBC comedy *Absolutely Fabulous* called 'Sex' the following year.

He made fleeting appearances in other popular TV shows including *Bramwell*, *The Bill*, *Degrees of Error*, *Ruth Rendell Mysteries* and *Crocodile Shoes*. These small roles were keeping him busy as a jobbing actor but he was far from well known and never felt he could relax for long. In 1997, the long-running Channel 5 soap *Family Affairs* offered him a part among the original cast, as pub regular Tim Webster. Although many of the show's actors would go on to greater things, Idris has enjoyed by far the most success.

But of course at that time he could have no idea what lay ahead, and, while this steady flow of small parts was paying the rent, it was nowhere near enough to fulfil his burning ambition.

It was only when he was cast as a regular on the acclaimed sci-fi series *Ultraviolet*, playing soldier Vaughan Rice, who was a member of a secret government vampire-hunting squad, that he really started to believe he could make a career out of acting. Only six episodes of *Ultraviolet* were made, but the show gathered a cult following and was aired in the US.

He also went on to play forensic scientist Matt Gregory in the BBC drama *Dangerfield*, and appeared in detective drama *The Inspector Lynley Mysteries*. However, Idris knew his heart lay in movies, but during his time in London he only managed to land a handful of minor film roles. The first, in 1997, was a short South African film called *Behind The Mask*, in which he played Ovronramwen. Two years later, he had the chance to appear alongside legendary actress Catherine Deneuve, as Grégoire in the French comedy *Belle Maman*. However, he was slowly starting to become a familiar face, and within a year had been cast alongside Matthew Rhys and Sienna Guillory in *Sorted*, a gritty feature film about a young lawyer investigating his brother's mysterious death, only to uncover the seedier side of the London club scene.

With *Belle Maman*, his first feature film under his belt, Idris felt the time was right to tackle the big time once again. He had sufficient experience, he felt, to take on the American movie-making machine. And so, in 1999, America beckoned again: 'I had a love affair with New York from the time I was 19, from when I decided that acting was gonna be it for me,' he said.

He was convinced that, if he was to stand a chance of making it in the world of acting, he needed to be in America. 'If you go to Africa and you're white, you're probably not going to get much work either,' he admitted. 'But the fact is that there is a longer history of black integration in the US. I don't have any resentment about this: I did the maths, calculated it against my ambition and decided to leave England.'

At the age of 27, determined to fulfil his ambition, Idris returned to New York. Idris had found himself increasingly frustrated at the lack of roles for black actors in Britain, and so he joined an exodus that would also include Marianne Jean-Baptiste, Adrian Lester, Marsha Thomason, David Harewood and Thandie Newton heading across the Atlantic.

However, this time he was not alone for he had the added responsibility of his wife Hanne,. She supported his move to the States, and believed he would make a success of it. They did not make the move on a whim; he was a man with a clear mission in mind. Despite the grave reservations expressed by their families, the couple sold their house in London, making a clean £60,000 profit, and jetted off to start a new life in Brooklyn.

'I was working all the time,' Idris explains. '*Silent Witness*, *Family Affairs*, *Insiders*, *Dangerfield* – I'd done loads of work in a short space of time. I got a Range Rover and a three-bedroom house and I'm married. Nothing was bad for me.

'I couldn't say that I had a horrible time as an actor, a black actor, here. But what I will say is that it just wasn't fulfilling my ambition. I was like, "What next?" I wanted to be on a bigger stage. In England there's only so much work for actors, period, never mind if you're black. So I was like, nah man, I want to be with Denz and them, Wesley and them. Those were my idols. Denz, Wesley and Taye Diggs.'

With the pressure mounting from all sides, he was more determined than ever that this time he would make his dreams come true. On the other side of the Atlantic, he was certain there would be more roles for a black actor. But the American Dream did not come true fast enough for his liking, and life in the States proved tougher than even he had imagined in his worst nightmares. Within a year, all their savings were gone, and Idris's promising television career was floundering. What would later prove to be his greatest asset was now his Achilles heel – he could not pull off a convincing American accent.

Since his visa would not allow him to do any other work besides acting, Idris would periodically pop back to the UK for small parts, and when he was in New York he would hit the streets looking for work that paid in cash.

He finally got a break in a downtown nightclub called Ludlow: 'There was an East Village DJ called Greg Paul, who was playing all this UK garage,' Idris recalled. 'I was like, "What do you know about all that?" And he's like, "Man, I love So Solid Crew." I'm talking back then. So I said, "You got a mic back there?"

'I'm like, "Bidda-bidda-bop to the ones and the twos..." I'm not saying anything but this guy thinks I'm spitting off the top, like Jay-Z. So he goes, "Hey do you DJ?" And boom, I was in! That's how I survived in New York.'

Many people in New York still remember Idris from those days, and recognise him as the guy from the clubs, not the movies.

'It's funny because New York remembers me, before I do what I do now,' he says. 'It's like going back to East London. I meet people all the time who say, "Yo, man, weren't you that DJ, though?"'

Although he finally had an income of sorts, life back then was not easy for Idris. His wife Hanne was increasingly anxious about their future and the auditions were going badly. They moved to a cheaper apartment in Jersey City, but money was still tight and pretty soon the marriage began to fall apart. By 2001 his wife was pregnant, unable to work and struggling to settle in New York, away from her friends and family.

Gradually, the relationship broke down and the pair went

their separate ways – Hanne now lives in the city of Duluth, just outside Atlanta, with their 11-year-old daughter Isan, who Idris sees as often as he can. But at the time her decision to call time on their turbulent relationship, and to throw him out of their apartment still came as a shock: 'She didn't adjust to the culture as quickly as I did. We just had a hard time,' Idris explained. 'The next thing you know, we broke up.'

Although he and Hanne did not actually divorce until 2005, Idris now found himself alone and unemployed. Before long, he ended up homeless and struggling to survive; he had hit rock bottom. For Idris, it was the toughest time in his life: 'I was just making enough to put the lights on,' he admits. 'I'm like, "Right! Right, I'll do it by myself!" Jumped in my car. Nowhere to go, nowhere.

'I remember thinking I've gotta make something of myself here,' he went on. 'I just parked my car near where I lived. Thought about going upstairs, but the energy was so bad, so I slept in my car. That was a low point. And I did that for six weeks. Go home, take a shower, but there was nowhere to go.'

For three years, he admits, things were so bad he 'couldn't catch a cold': 'I mean, it was like, "Fuck, where did I go wrong? I had a lot of promise in England, you know. What the fuck are you doing here? Your visa's going to run out soon, you're going to have a baby, what the fuck are you doing? That's what's going through my head,' he explained.

'To me, going to America wasn't so much a risk. It was just, "Why not?" I teach this to my kid [Isan] all the time. I say, "Don't let anyone say you can't do it". That's been my mentality. And that has got me into trouble.

'Coming to America wasn't easy, I didn't just walk into a job. I had a lot of years with no job, no money. But I never gave up.'

But Idris's confidence is fireproof, his optimistic outlook

wholly American. He was always convinced he would get there in the end. But, after moving out of the flat he shared with Hanne, the future looked bleak. Alone and unable to find work, he ended up homeless and sleeping in his cheap brown Chevrolet van for weeks on end.

'The apartment we had lived in together was in Jersey City. So when I left I was sofa-hopping here and there and got to a place where I was parking the van in Jersey somewhere and just camping down for the night,' he explained. 'It was very tough back then – I couldn't get an acting job so I slept rough in my van for eight weeks. I took any job I could to earn money, but even so I never once buckled on acting; I know I would be nothing if I couldn't perform. Take that away and you take away my oxygen.'

Remaining focused on his ambition, and determined to succeed in a highly competitive world was not easy for Idris, and he still shudders when he looks back on some of the jobs he was forced to take during the three years of hardship he endured as he struggled to get his career off the ground.

Being 6ft 3in helped land him work as a bouncer at nightclubs and comedy clubs, but it was gruelling work, the hours were long and one night it almost cost him his life.

'Things happened my parents don't even know about,' he revealed. 'I worked as a bouncer at a place in the East Village and my friend got stabbed to death. It was a night I wasn't working. I lived in New York from 1999 to 2001. After 9/11 the city had its identity ripped up from underneath it. There was super-bad paranoia and it had this dangerous edge – there were a lot of incidents.

'I had a gun pointed at my head. It was one of those silly situations. I was on the door, there was this guy and suddenly there's a gun at my head. The crazy thing was, I wasn't so scared. I was really calm. I just talked my way out of it, told him to chill out. I just kept on talking. I looked him in the eye and said, "Come on, man, it's not this serious."

'I was more scared when Denzel Washington put a gun to my head [in *American Gangster*]. It's weird but the reality was less scary than the movie. In New York, I knew he had a bullet in the gun and, if he pulled it, I would be dead. I think my natural defence was to believe it would be OK.'

Working as a doorman back then gave Idris direct access to Manhattan's seedy underbelly, and to boost his meagre income he even found himself selling drugs on the street. 'You got to remember I was hustling back then,' he went on. 'And I mean huss-ell-ing. I was working the door at Caroline's comedy club. Selling weed, 10 spots, everything, just to make money because the acting weren't coming in fast enough.

'I was running with cats. I mean, I was DJing, but I was also pushing bags of weed, I was doing my work; I had to. I know that sounds corny, but this is the truth.'

While he was risking everything selling drugs, Idris had to endure the sight of other more successful stars such as Dave Chappelle walking past him without a glance: 'All those black comedians, they knew me as a doorman,' he sighed.

He also earned extra cash appearing in music videos for Fat Joe, Angie Stone and English rapper Giggs. And, between shifts, he raced to as many auditions as he could possibly manage. Like numerous other actors before him, all he managed was small bit parts in shows requiring many extras, such as NBC's hit legal drama *Law & Order*. He said, 'I was on a well-beaten path of actors – what we all call "the *Law & Order* route". I spent two years auditioning for everything and then *The Wire* came up.'

Although he did not know it, those dark days of pushing drugs and dealing with gun-toting clubbers would soon be nothing more than a dark and distant memory for Idris.

CHAPTER SIX

THE BIG BREAK

Idris knew that simply living in America and turning up to auditions was not going to be enough; to beat the competition, he would need to reinvent himself entirely. Despite finding himself homeless, broke and alone, he was so determined to reach the big time that he immersed himself in the local community until he felt he could convincingly pass himself off as a genuine American, born and bred.

'I knew that, if I wanted to be all I could be, I would have to go to the US,' he explained. 'It took three years to get the accent right.'

Idris worked relentlessly on perfecting his American accent, by listening attentively to the men around him as they talked. And, while he studied, he won a small role in the ill-fated movie *Buffalo Soldiers* alongside Joaquin Phoenix. Although a step in the right direction, it was not quite enough and he began to worry that the situation for black actors was just as dire in America as he had found it back in Britain.

Idris knew there were not enough opportunities for him at

home: 'In England, although it is very multi-cultural and multi-racial and stuff, for an Afro-Caribbean on television there was not as much as we'd like to see. But the politics of a black man getting a job is the same all over the world.

'I didn't get to America and it was gravy; in fact, I didn't work for four years, partly because my accent was terrible.'

Just as he was starting to wonder if he would have to beg for his old job back at the factory, everything changed. He won the part of Achilles in a 2001 stage production of *Troilus and Cressida*.

'He was banging it out here, *Dangerfield*, *Family Affairs*,' said Elba's British agent Roger Charteris. 'But when he moved to New York an actor dropped out of Peter Hall's *Troilus and Cressida* and we managed to get him an audition for that.'

Casting director Alex L. Fogel had seen him in the London production of *Troilus and Cressida*, and said, 'I see something phenomenal in him.'

Charteris added: 'Those sort of opportunities don't happen here. We don't take people who are at that level and say, "Go fly with the eagles". We say, "Fly with the pigeons, and do that for a while before you go anywhere".'

Idris will always remember 4 January 2002 as the day that changed his life. That was the day, thanks to Fogel, when he managed to land himself an audition with Hollywood producer David Simon for a forthcoming HBO show called *The Wire*. As far as Idris was concerned, this was his very last shot at the big time, for he knew that time was running out for him, and his confidence was slowly starting to crack.

'It was just another audition,' Idris said. But it was truly make or break and his chance of success rested entirely on whether or not he could pull off a convincing accent. 'I lived in America for a long time before I started working as an actor,' Idris recalled.

'Some actors show up on set and have never done an American accent before, so they rely on a slew of mechanisms. Part of what makes an accent is understanding why people speak that way – you have to understand the culture.'

While he was out of work, Idris had done his best to remain upbeat and optimistic, and had worked tirelessly on perfecting his accent. Unable to afford a dialect coach, he had improvised and made frequent visits to a barber's called Ace of Spades near his home in Fort Greene, Brooklyn.

'I was living in Flatbush – remember the Ace of Spades barbershop? They used to call me "English",' he recalled. 'I was like, "I'm trying to get this accent down, do you mind if I just sit in the barbershop and talk?" And that was it, man. When you got niggers snapping on you and shit, you can't come back with the rebuttals in an English accent. It's not quick enough. They'd be like, "What you say, nigger? The Queen ain't up in here. Ain't nobody can understand you." So you know, I'd just have to get into it.'

Despite the teasing from the older men, Idris remained completely focused on his mission, working as hard as he could on perfecting a convincing American accent.

He remembers a day when he strutted into the Ace of Spades, proudly wearing an expensive new Avirex jacket, known as an AV, which he could ill afford. He was also wearing Timberland boots and Levi's jeans, but the guys in the barbers were not impressed by what he thought was a sharp new look: 'I had a proper black-on-black AV, a fresh pair of Tims and, because I'm from London, I had the Levi's straight cut,' Idris recalled. 'But when I walked into the Ace of Spades, these niggers clowned the fuck out of me because of my jeans. Avirex jackets make you look really big, that's the thing. So they were like, "Nigger, what the fuck? We got Avirex on toothpicks in this motherfucker!"'

While many English actors trying to make it big in America preserve their Englishness as a point of difference, and use their accent to land specific roles, Idris was determined to be seamlessly transatlantic. He was constantly studying the American accent, regardless of the dead-end jobs he found himself forced into in order to make ends meet. He explained: 'Because I worked everywhere, in nightclubs, as a bouncer, I got the accent down. If you can fool a New York cab driver into thinking you're American, you can fool anyone. Just because I wasn't working as an actor didn't mean I wasn't working – I was absorbing.'

And he became so absorbed that he never let his finely tuned accent slip throughout the gruelling audition process.

'One of the interesting things about me is that I can talk to anyone and fit in almost anywhere,' said Idris. 'It's something I've been doing for more than 10,000 hours, as [controversial journalist] Malcolm Gladwell would say.

'I can read people, work out if they'll like me or not. It gets better with age because less is expected and I can smell bullshit from much, much further away. I don't even have to get close to smell it! Now, I can see them coming. In my early days, I could walk into a casting director's room and, coupled with the fact that I've got some talent, I'm going to get that part. I had it down almost to a science in England. Wasn't as good at it in America, though,' he laughed.

At the time he heard about the audition for *The Wire*, Idris was under immense pressure to give up on acting altogether. Although Hanne had thrown him out, she was just weeks away from giving birth and he was determined to be involved in his baby's life.

He said: 'I'd had three or four years of unemployment, not getting acting jobs. I was watching Denzel Washington and Wesley Snipes and saying, "I can do that. I can be right there with them." My wife was about eight and a half months pregnant; if I didn't get it, I was going to have to leave the US. We knew that, if I didn't have acting work after my daughter was born, we would be up shit street.

'My ambition is what took me out to the States. I wanted to achieve something that hadn't been achieved; I wanted to avoid stereotypes. But that meant this was gonna be a slow-burn career.'

Initially, Idris read for the part of Baltimore drug kingpin Avon Barksdale, and was asked to return four times until the producers finally made a decision, although they had no idea how excruciating the wait was for him, nor how desperate he was for work: 'I was studying in my van for the auditions,' he said.

He did four auditions over a period of two months, and finally, on the day his daughter was born in 2002, the producers decided to give Idris the role of Russell 'Stringer' Bell, Barksdale's less prominent business manager. But in his final audition when they asked which part of America he was originally from, Idris left the producers stunned when he spoke to them in his normal British accent.

'I remember [creator] David Simon asked me on the last one, "Where in the US are you from?" This whole time I've been talking in an American accent. And I was like, "If I fucking lie right now, I'm going to lose this shit". So I said, "Listen, guys, I'm English, I'm from East London, man."

'David was like, "Wow! Get the fuck out of here!" I thought I'd pissed him off but he was really impressed. He said, "Listen, you got a good accent but we can't offer you Avon Barksdale. What about Stringer?" I said, "Who?"

'Stringer had, like, ten lines. I thought, "Just give me a job, I don't give a fuck. It's a pilot. I knew I was going to get a cheque, as long as I was a season regular. He said, "You got it."'

He had convinced the people who mattered that he was born and raised in the US. All those long days spent studying and listening to talk at his local barber's shop while he looked for acting work had been worth it, and the gamble of moving across the Atlantic had finally paid off too. But Idris was in no position to celebrate his success. On the day of the last audition, Hanne had just gone into labour and he needed to rush her straight into Christ Hospital in New Jersey. But, determined not to miss out on any potential earnings, he dropped her off at the maternity ward and headed out to DJ at a club called Silver (at the time DJing was his only source of income). The couple were separated but Hanne still understood Idris needed to take whatever work came his way.

At last, Idris had the break he had been waiting for, but he nearly blew it by getting pulled over for drunk driving in the early hours as he raced back to see his newborn baby.

'So I played the gig,' he said. 'I told everyone, "Yo, I booked a pilot!" And everyone was celebrating. My boss Danny bought a bottle of champagne, and he gave me a bit of extra money on top of my usual. So I had nearly $300 when I was driving home in my Astro van – it was a good night! But, man, I was so liquored up. There was this half-drunk bottle of Hennessy in the back and I'm like this, going through the Holland Tunnel.

'And just as I came out, just when I saw the Christ Hospital up ahead, that's when I heard it – whup, whup!'

To his horror, the police were right behind him, pulling him over.

'That's what saved me,' he explained. 'As I pressed my brakes, the Henny bottle rolled off the back and under the seat. And when the guy knocked on the window and said, "Licence and registration," he saw the band on my wrist. He said, "You been to hospital?" I said, "No, sir, that's for my wife who's about to give birth any minute. I'm a DJ, I'm just coming back from a gig."'

Somehow, it worked. The police officer let Idris go and he managed to reach the hospital just in time to see his daughter Isan being born at 4.49am. He has a tattoo on his forearm to mark the moment. It was to start a love affair with tattoos, which adorn his body: 'They're all personal,' he explained. 'My daughter's name is on this arm and my granddad's name is on this arm; there are philosophies of songs that I love.

'Body art for me, man, is a fucking form of expression of the highest order. This is our canvas, our container; these are our bricks. All this is designed to hold up this one little device called the brain and I just want to decorate it and be proud of it. I've got a shit memory; I can only remember lines.

'But I look at this and I won't forget it. My industry is full of gas and I don't want to get derailed.'

From that moment on, life improved. Idris had a salary and a baby daughter he adored – although he never managed to patch up his marriage.

The bleak portrayal of both cops and drug dealers has led *The Wire* to be lauded by critics and audiences as one of the best TV shows in history from the moment it aired on the premium cable network HBO on 2 June 2002. By the time the show ended, after five seasons and sixty episodes, on 9 March 2008, Elba's star status was firmly established. His role quickly expanded as the show took off and the writers nuanced Bell's brooding character – Stringer took economics classes, ran dealer meetings with parliamentary rules and plotted with quiet, cold-blooded resolve to break out of the tough under-world he inhabited, to exploit the corruption in the legitimate business and political community.

He was no ordinary right-hand man. As well as being ultraviolent, Stringer also strived to improve himself – he read Adam Smith's *The Wealth of Nations* and had lofty ambitions to take over not just Baltimore's drug trade, but also its undervalued waterfront property and he planned to control several biddable local politicians.

Idris could not believe his luck had finally changed: 'It was a massive achievement at that time,' he admitted. 'Here I was in America, on an HBO show! I was like, "Fuck off!" I didn't have a massive part in the first series, but I was living my dream. It came after a long stint of unemployment, at a point when I really wanted to do it. I threw my heart into it.'

Each season focused on corruption in a different area of the city of Baltimore, from the drug trade to local government and the print news media, and the effect institutions have on individuals who are committed to them.

Despite receiving only fairly modest ratings, not casting any big-name stars and never winning major television awards, *The Wire* gathered a huge cult following and has been described as one of the most accomplished works of fiction, thanks to its realistic portrayal of urban life and its deep exploration of society and politics.

The show's creator, and former police reporter at *The Baltimore Sun*, David Simon, had often been frustrated by the bureaucracy of the Baltimore police department and based the script on his own experiences. He said: 'We are not selling hope, or audience gratification, or cheap victories with this show. *The Wire* is making an argument about what institutions – bureaucracies, criminal enterprises, the cultures of addiction, raw capitalism even – do to individuals. It is not designed purely as entertainment. It is, I'm afraid, a somewhat angry show.'

But executives at the television network NBC disliked the

show's pessimism so Simon took it to HBO – for whom he had already written a miniseries called *The Corner*.

Before the show aired, Simon warned the Mayor of Baltimore that he would be giving a bleak portrayal of the city, and would feature several prominent real-life Baltimore figures in cameo roles – including former Maryland Governor Robert L. Ehrlich Jnr, former police chief Ed Norris and a former mayor. The Mayor later admitted to being a fan of the show, which many called a love letter to the city.

The show was so realistic there were even reports of real criminals watching it to learn how to counter police investigation techniques, and the fifth season's portrayal of a working newsroom has been hailed as the most realistic portrayal of the media in film and television.

Idris relished his first major role. For the first time in his career, he had a reason to be proud and actually congratulated himself for sticking with his dream: 'Getting *The Wire*, going from not having a job to getting a massive job on HBO, was one of the best moments of my life. That's much bigger than getting a pat on the back for a performance because it's part of your personal journey.'

He threw himself wholeheartedly into the role of Stringer Bell, and for many fans he was the best thing about the show, even though he could often be ruthless and unlikeable. But the writers built up Stringer until he ultimately betrayed his boss. Idris said: 'I knew the writing was special and I knew that, with them trying to tackle a problem like that on a major HBO show, then it had to have some legs.

'It turns out that it really has had some legs! It changed my life, of course. I blame it all on *The Wire*!'

However, the show was slow to gather popularity: 'It's actually quite criminal how *The Wire* was systematically ignored,' Idris said. 'Stringer is very calculating and he has to be for so many reasons. He'll calculate the next steps, shipments, inventory, pays workers, all that. But the wicked part is that he can plan murders because that's a part of his business.

'I'll tell you, if I, Idris, had to contract for murders as part of my job, I couldn't do it because I have a heart. I have no stomach for ordering other people's deaths. Stringer just gets in there, orders the deed and bam, that's it, done and he doesn't think twice about it.

'There's no way I could be that cold. I'm also a more lively kid out there, doing stuff and I can't just do one thing forever. Stringer is committed to his job and business, so much so he doesn't have much of a personal life so he's more one-dimensional.

'As for me, I have a child, a life, a thirst for travel, you know, I'm curious, whereas Stringer is more interested in being the best business person and his interests don't go further than that.'

Idris admitted later that he got so caught up in his role as a drug dealer that he would even smoke marijuana with his co-star Wood Harris in between takes while filming the show between 2002 and 2004. 'Wood is a big burner [pot smoker], proper,' he revealed. 'We'd sit in the trailer going over these very complex scenes and he'd burn all the time.

'One scene was pushed back and we sat in the trailer, burning and burning and playing music. The next thing you know, we're on the set, high as a kite. But it was one of the best scenes you've ever seen in your life.'

Since the majority of the cast was African-American, accurately reflecting the demographics of Baltimore, local schools and colleges would study the show, and students told how it had 'hit a nerve' with the black community, and they knew real-life counterparts of many of the characters.

Idris himself was fascinated by his role in the show: 'The

characters are complex,' he said. 'Stringer Bell has a very different complexity, and the writing makes that character fantastic.

'The part itself on paper doesn't say anything. When I read it, it was the guy who stands next to Avon. If there is any complexity to be found in that character, it's a combination of the writers and myself saying, "Let's dig a little deeper, let's dig beneath the surface a little."'

Elba's business-minded character Stringer Bell paid the ultimate price for betraying Barksdale in the third series, but by then the role had transformed the actor's life and given him huge credibility with a new audience who were electrified by his performance. And he admits that he drew on a wealth of personal experience for the role, having experimented with illegal drugs in the past. 'I'm not gonna lie, I've tried everything,' he admitted. 'I've tried it all. I played one of the biggest drug dealers in the world on TV, so you think I'd know what I was talking about.

'I live within club culture, so I've done everything that goes with that. I'm obviously not an addict! But I have experimented.'

Idris understands the show's enduring popularity: 'I think *The Wire* is relatable. It reflects an on-going issue across America, about inaccuracies in major cities between rich and the poor and some of the things that go on behind the red tape of council and government bodies.'

Although some of the storylines may have been rather close to home, the show was given an enormous boost when the President of the United States, Barack Obama, said *The Wire* was his favourite television series, and after a visit to The White House in 2012, at which the leader of the free world asked Idris to sit next to him, the actor excitedly tweeted: 'The President let me know I was his second favourite character in *The Wire*.'

The *Guardian* newspaper hailed *The Wire* as possibly the

greatest show of the last 20 years. TV critic Charlie Brooker described it as 'The best TV show since the invention of radio'. The show was nominated for a huge variety of awards including the Primetime Emmy Awards, the Television Critics Association Awards and Writers Guild of America Awards. Schools and universities, including Harvard Law School, have run courses on *The Wire* in disciplines ranging from law to sociology.

In Britain, the University of York's head of sociology Roger Burrows said the show 'makes a fantastic contribution to their understanding of contemporary urbanism and is a contrast to dry, dull, hugely expensive studies that people carry out on the same issues'.

The show was broadcast around the world, dubbed into several languages, including Norwegian, German, Hungarian and Dutch, although Idris had already left the show by then and did not earn any extra money when it was sold around the globe.

'I enjoy seeing the reach of it,' said Elba. 'I'll go to a press junket and there'll be a guy from London and a guy from Taiwan who are both hardcore *Wire* fans, and that to me is enjoyable. So I've always liked talking about it. I've faced criticism before from people who say, "Oh, you don't really speak highly enough of *The Wire*." I do, I love *The Wire*. I was written out of the show early, so it's a different sort of journey for me.'

Fans were devastated when his character was killed off in episode 11 of Season 3. Around Idris's home at the time, in New Jersey, Stringer Bell had become something of a local hero. A crowd of his neighbours came to the house, shouting up at the windows, 'You kidding me, man? Yo, why you ain't tell us, String?' Idris said: 'I remember when Stringer Bell died – man, the neighbourhood knew I was there. They fucking camped outside my house!'

But, even after the death of his character, Idris remained philosophical about the role that made his name: 'I played Stringer at a time of my career when I'd moved to the States and I wasn't working,' he said. 'I couldn't get a job for about four years, so Stringer was my lifeline, I played Stringer for about three years.

'My relationship with the character is that first of all it changed my life but everywhere I go there are still huge Stringer fans, and it wows me that the writing and the characters touched so many people.

'What happens to Stringer in the end, there is a certain sequence that he goes through in the third season, and I remember David Simon and I had a conversation about it, and I had to fight. He had a certain idea about how Stringer should go out and I was on the same page with him. Stringer should go out, but how?

'Of course, when you've worked on a character for three years, you feel in part responsible for what happens to him.'

Elba's role was lauded as a standout performance from a cast of hundreds and guaranteed him star status, and his pick of quality TV and movie roles, although he was keen not to be typecast as a 'black gangster'.

'You wouldn't describe other actors by their ethnicity,' he explained. 'You just describe them as actors. The word "black" is associated with something negative so, as soon as you say it, you're casting some sort of shadow on whatever it is.

'I could have played Stringer Bell-type characters forever. I could be on the telly right now, in my own show, earning 150 grand an episode.'

But Idris turned down parts offered to him by the major US networks, which he saw as variations on the same cool charismatic gangster.

'Let's imagine Stringer Bell opens a real estate agency,' he mused. 'He's a real estate agent – but he's got an edge about him. I just didn't accept any more roles as gangsters.

'For about two years after playing Stringer, I had an identity crisis, I didn't know what my own accent was,' he joked.

Although his career has gone from strength to strength, for Idris, few scripts have matched the quality of *The Wire*.

He added: 'But the truth is, the films coming my way do not bear any resemblance to the writing I've been accustomed and privileged to do – *The Wire* obviously being the flagship of that.'

The show won him so many famous fans that he started to rub shoulders with big-name urban artists he had admired for years, such as P. Diddy, Ludacris and Jay-Z. He even ended up co-producing and recording a spoken word intro on Jay-Z's 2008 album, *American Gangster*. And he found a following among real drug dealers, who leapt at the chance to initiate conversations with him in public.

'Wherever I go, the real hard-core drug dealers come up to me and confide in me. I almost feel guilty turning around and saying, "'Ello, mate, my name's Idris and I'm from London." I don't want to break the illusion,' he said.

Despite the phenomenal global success of the show, which still has a huge cult following years after it ended, Idris has never actually sat through an entire episode. 'By the way,' he says, 'you know I've never watched *The Wire*. I've seen a full episode at screenings but never at home. I've never watched an entire season. I've not seen any episode of Season Two, most of Season Three and none of Seasons Four and Five. I'm supercritical of my own work. As an actor, if you're being told how wonderful you are, what do you strive for? I don't know if I'm good just because some critic says I am in the press.'

Regardless of what the press say, Idris is only too aware of when he has done well because the fans will make sure he knows, in no uncertain terms.

'I didn't realise how popular *The Wire* had become in the UK,' he admits. 'I came home and I was getting chased down the street.'

But he knows that, whatever the future holds, everyone will always remember it was playing Stringer Bell in *The Wire* that gave him his big break, and for that he remains eternally grateful.

'That really is more about the writing of *The Wire* than it is the performance,' he says with typical modesty. 'You know, Stringer Bell is a great character that was written. I happened to play him, but it could have been anybody playing that role.

'I think I brought Stringer to life my way, but *The Wire* isn't a classic because of Stringer Bell. *The Sopranos* was a classic because of Tony Soprano.'

The Wire, which also made a star of fellow Brit Dominic West (Detective Jimmy McNulty), may have finished in 2008, but it still makes a good calling card for Idris.

CHAPTER SEVEN

HOLLYWOOD COMES CALLING

After the phenomenal success of *The Wire*, Idris knew there was no turning back. Making the move across the Atlantic to America had paid off, and he was in no hurry to return home.

He was still burning with ambition and felt he had much further to go: 'I'm an ambitious person,' he said. 'I never consider myself in competition with anyone, and I'm not saying that from an arrogant standpoint, it's just that my journey started so, so long ago, and I'm still on it and I won't stand still.'

Although he was not quite established as a star, he felt, as a black actor, more opportunities would come his way in the States.

A contemporary of Idris's from those days, Paul McKenzie, who went on to edit the black lifestyle magazine *Essence*, had given up on the acting business after being invited to audition as a criminal for *Crimewatch*. According to him, Idris should not have had to move away from Britain to get his break.

'It is such a shame for an actor as talented as Idris to have to go to America to make his name,' McKenzie declared. 'It is getting better, but we often say it and we're not whingeing –

black people are massively under-represented on TV, and the roles that are written for us are incredibly narrow.'

Despite the obstacles in his path, McKenzie remains a huge fan of Elba's, and says his readership love him too: 'He's got presence, he's got charm, he's a bloody good actor and he's English. He just ticks all the boxes,' he said.

'There are actors, whatever their colour, who guys want to be and girls want to sleep with. From a guy's point of view, there are people, actors or sports stars or whoever – who, if your girlfriend left you for him, you'd hold the door and understand it. He is definitely one.'

While McKenzie took another path, Idris always stayed entirely focused on his goal. And at last a broad array of scripts were coming his way and he was able to land himself a string of minor but lucrative roles in Hollywood hits, which would firmly establish him as a star of the big screen.

Although Idris's face was by this point gracing DVD box sets across the world thanks to his towering performance in *The Wire*, he was determined not to be typecast. 'It was easy,' he said. 'I just didn't accept any more roles as gangsters.'

In 2005, shortly after leaving the series that gave him his big break, Idris signed his first significant role: *Sometimes in April*, an historical drama film made for television about the Rwandan genocide of 1994. Idris played Captain Augustin Muganza, an officer in the Rwandan army who witnessed the killing of close to 800,000 people in 100 days, including some of his own family.

The film, which aired on HBO, was noted for its gruesome and graphic portrayal of the brutal violence as people struggled to survive the genocide, and the aftermath as they tried to find justice and reconciliation.

He managed to land himself a role playing Paul in an episode of the American sitcom *Girlfriends* in 2005 but, while the series ran for years, Idris's character only appeared in the first episode. To his frustration, the show did not get much attention. *The Gospel* came next and proved to be the ideal film for Idris to shed his Stringer Bell persona. He played the egotistical Reverend Charles Frank, whose vision for his church causes a rift between himself and the dying bishop's pop star son. Although the film itself was not much of a hit, Idris was nominated for Best Actor in the Black Reel Awards of 2006 and the part immediately led him on to bigger and better things.

He was gathering a small but loyal army of fans and was dubbed one of the Ten Hottest Men on the Planet in 2004 and 2005 by *Essence* magazine, which did him no harm with casting directors, or women either. And the work was coming in thick and fast for Idris. British director Jim O'Hanlon managed to lure Idris back across the Atlantic once again to appear in his British football drama *All In The Game*, where he was looking for an actor with enough charisma to go toe to toe with tough-guy actor Ray Winstone, and Idris fitted the bill perfectly: 'He's a very beautiful man,' said O'Hanlon. 'And he just has that presence and confidence that very beautiful people have. The big thing with Idris is presence – that is the big word, both as an actor and as a person. He often has fewer lines than anyone else, but you still feel he has the bigger part, because he's luminous.'

Despite his swagger, which has led him to strike up friendships with superstars Beyoncé and Jay-Z, O'Hanlon added that what is most surprising about Idris is actually his reserve: 'He's not a showy actor,' he said later. 'You see in *No. 1 Ladies' Detective Agency*, he does so much with his eyes, how he looks at people, how he listens to people.

'I think he could be huge. He looks like a star, and he comes across as a star, and, if you are going to be a major player in

Hollywood, that is one of the qualities you need. But, of course, it's backed up in Idris's case with being a fantastic actor.'

O'Hanlon's prediction was to come true, although perhaps not as fast as Idris himself would have liked. He was not out of work for long, however. Next up was a meaty role in the touching romantic drama *Daddy's Little Girls*. Idris was thrilled when he got the call confirming he was to play the part of Monty James, a hard-working blue-collar car mechanic who falls in love with a wealthy lawyer while she is helping him regain custody of his three daughters. But the budding romance and his hopes of winning back his children are threatened by the return of his ex. The role gave him the opportunity he had longed for to shake off Stringer Bell once and for all, and to completely reinvent himself as an actor who can play a diverse range of parts.

'I would never be fearful of any character,' he said. 'I think there's a tendency for actors like myself, and I don't mean to generalise myself, but I've played "men's men" if you will, characters that are simmering rage and calculated.

'There's a trend not to play anything that is opposed to that. When I left Stringer, one of the films I did was Tyler Perry's *Daddy's Little Girls*, which was about a man doting over his three little girls. I remember there was talk, "Why? Why would you do that? Play gangsters. Play ruthless."

'It's really funny because the same people who loved me as Stringer Bell were the same people that were watching *Daddy's Little Girls* literally in tears. Some people don't like the film, but some of the guys that came up to me and said, "Yo, I want to see you play gangsters" were the same ones that were in tears because they either had strained relationships with their children, or they loved their children so much and they were watching a character that they could relate to.

'I don't mind playing characters that are opposite of what people think I am.'

Although it gave Elba a chance to show his softer side, the film, which opened on Valentine's Day 2007, was not a hit. It made $31 million worldwide, making it writer and director Tyler Perry's lowest-grossing movie, and received generally negative reviews from critics, although Idris did receive a nomination in the Best Actor category for the role at the 2007 BET Awards.

But Idris later fell out with Tyler Perry when he criticised the trend for the cross-dressing of black characters – a phenomenon many movie-goers would recognise from *The Klumps* and *Big Momma's House* – describing it as 'buffoonish'. Regardless of the controversy, for his role in *Daddy's Little Girls*, Idris was nominated for a BET Award for Actor of the Year. But at the awards ceremony he was infuriated when asked to justify his earlier comments by a reporter called DC Livers from Black Press Radio: 'Can I justify my comments on Tyler Perry? No, it's all explained. Everything you need. It's all self-explanatory,' he said.

He then left the stage, muttering 'Bitch' under his breath and refusing to answer any further questions.

Idris also went on to tackle the controversial subject of under-representation of black actors in Hollywood: 'Imagine a film such as *Inception* with an entire cast of black people,' he said. 'Do you think it would be successful? Would people watch it? But no one questions the fact that everyone's white. That's what we have to change.'

The same year, he appeared as Ben in *The Reaping*, a horror movie also starring Hilary Swank. The pair played scientists investigating claims of a miracle by a priest in Chile, where a river has turned red. They uncover a cache of hazardous waste illegally stashed in an underground oil well, which ruptured, giving the biological effects of a miracle.

Production, which took place in Louisiana, was delayed when Hurricane Katrina struck, and the film's release was postponed several times. Again, Idris had another flop on his hands, as the movie was widely panned by critics. Rotten Tomatoes called it: 'Schlocky, spiritually shallow and scare free'. However, just weeks after *The Reaping* failed to make a mark at the box office, Idris's next film was released: *28 Weeks Later*, sequel to Danny Boyle's post-apocalyptic horror film *28 Days Later*. In joining the cast of Juan Carlos Fresnadillo's zombie movie, it was the first time Idris had appeared in a well-received film, for which he was nominated for Best Actor at the BET Awards in 2008.

He played Stone, a soldier struggling to stop the spread of the rage virus that had wiped out most of the population. In the aftermath, just a handful of survivors are left struggling to escape the infection in an abandoned London.

The director said: 'We were quite taken aback by the phenomenal success of the first film, particularly in America. We saw an opportunity to make a second film that already had a built-in audience. We thought it would be a great idea to try and satisfy that audience again.'

Idris was delighted to return to London for filming, which mostly took place around his home in East London, and the film was hyped with an effective viral advertising campaign, which saw removable chalk powder graffiti sprayed in locations around London and Birmingham featuring the web address 'ragevirus.com'. There was also a popular graphic novel released to coincide with the release, a video game and a massive competition to win props from the set.

Reviews were positive, with most critics agreeing it lived up to the success of the original, and altogether the film grossed £64.2 million worldwide.

Plans for another sequel, *28 Months Later*, have been on hold since October 2010, when writer Alex Garland revealed: 'When we made *28 Days Later* the rights were frozen between a group of people who are no longer talking to each other. And so the film is never going to happen until those people start talking to each other. There is no script as far as I'm aware.'

Also in 2007, Idris was thrilled when he finally had the chance to fulfil one of his long-held ambitions, to work with one of his all-time heroes Denzel Washington, after landing a minor role as crime boss Tango in *American Gangster*. The Ridley Scott crime drama, which also starred Russell Crowe and another of Idris's idols, Cuba Gooding Jnr, was based on the career of a real-life gangster. Frank Lucas from North Carolina smuggled heroin into the United States on services planes returning from Vietnam.

Thanks to its all-star cast, critics raved about the movie when it opened in November 2007, grossing over $266.5 million worldwide. It was nominated for 21 awards, including two Oscars for Best Art Direction and Best Supporting Actress. And, although Idris only had a small role, and knew it would be tough to shine alongside industry heavyweights like Washington and Crowe, he gave a critically acclaimed performance, and many agree one of the best scenes in the film is when his character Tango was killed by Washington.

He was honoured to have the chance to work with legendary director Ridley Scott: 'Ridley is a mastermind at making films,' he said. 'It's like being in school – "This is what I am shooting and this is how I am going to use it".'

But after that Idris was determined not to play any more 'thug' roles and told the press at the National Association of

Black Owned Broadcasters, 'Denzel Washington is the last person to shoot me [with a gun] in a movie.'

With that in mind, Idris moved swiftly on to a production of a comedy drama called *This Christmas*, although he still played a familiar role, as the cool and conniving Quentin Whitfield. Starring Chris Brown, Mekhi Phifer and Loretta Devine, the film is about a family whose eldest son returns home for Christmas for the first time in four years. Idris's performance was widely praised and the movie brought in nearly $50 million at the box office in 2007.

In 2008, Idris seized the opportunity to fly out to Botswana to work on *The No. 1 Ladies' Detective Agency*, a TV comedy drama adapted from the best-selling novels by Alexander McCall Smith. With heavyweight writers Richard Curtis and Anthony Minghella writing the scripts, and with Hollywood hotshots Bob and Harvey Weinstein producing the series, the collaboration between the BBC and HBO was pretty much guaranteed to be a smash hit.

Idris was cast as Charlie Gotso, an adversary to the lead detective Mma Ramotswe, in whose Mercedes a collection of human bones is discovered. Starring opposite Jill Scott and Anika Noni Rose, he was excited to see how heavily promoted the show was back home in the UK. Although it received 6.3 million viewers, critics panned the production, with a reviewer from the *Guardian* summing it up as '*Heartbeat* basically, relocated to Botswana, a beautiful African country where smiley happy people, cardboard cut-out characters, go about their business with good humour, hard work, morality and diligence'.

Audiences did not share the producers' enthusiasm either, and the show was cancelled after its first season. Undaunted, almost immediately, he went on to work with his co-star Jessica Stroup in his next film, *Prom Night*, playing a police detective who discovers that the man who killed the parents of a local girl has escaped from prison. As Detective Winn, Idris is the hero of the film, who eventually tracks down and kills the murderer just as he tries to take his revenge.

Idris put in a solid performance and was excited to move straight on to his next project – Guy Ritchie's gangster heist *RocknRolla*. With a stellar cast including Gerard Butler and Thandie Newton, it hit the number-one spot as soon as it was released in the UK. Idris was nominated for a BET Award for Best Actor in 2009 for his role as Mumbles, partner to Scottish mobster One Two who leads a group of small-time crooks called the Wild Bunch.

In a similar film to his previous violent gangster films, *Lock, Stock and Two Smoking Barrels* and *Snatch*, Guy Ritchie handpicked each member of the cast. But Idris admitted afterwards that he is not a great fan of the director, who split from his wife Madonna soon after filming ended: 'He's a wanker,' said Idris. 'Guy's very calm and collected on the outside and he works extensively on trying to rid himself of any kind of angst. He has interesting people skills: he sort of engages with you and at the same time has his mind elsewhere.

'It was very surreal when his wife would show up. They were seemingly fine.'

After weeks of shooting with an entirely British cast in London, Idris was once again on a plane back to Los Angeles to film *The Human Contract*. A drama with Jada Pinkett Smith, the plot focuses on a successful but unhappy businessman who meets a free-spirited stranger who tempts him to be more reckless.

It was quickly becoming clear that Idris would never face a long period of unemployment again. He was working on back-to-back movies, barely having a chance to return to the UK to visit his family, but he was finally doing what he had always dreamt of and he dare not complain.

Next up was *The Unborn*, a supernatural horror film about a young woman tormented by a ghost, who seeks help from a Rabbi, played by Gary Oldman.

Idris played an Episcopal priest called Arthur Wyndham, who helped with an exorcism, but after being knocked unconscious gets possessed himself. The film was yet another huge flop, but it only made Idris more determined than ever to find himself bigger and better roles.

CHAPTER EIGHT

LEADING MAN

After a string of box-office disasters, Idris was more determined than ever to land himself a leading role. And his wish came true when he won his meatiest part so far in the hit thriller *Obsessed*, alongside the singer Beyoncé Knowles, who was appearing in her first major movie role.

Looking back on the shoot, Idris admitted it was quite a treat having to kiss the chart-topping singer, who is now married to his friend Jay-Z, as they played husband and wife in the film.

'That was a bit weird,' he recalled. 'We did a lot of the kissing scenes on day one of filming. I guess it was an ice breaker.'

Luckily, Beyoncé's rapper husband is not the jealous type: 'He's cool,' said Idris. 'We've worked together, there's a lot of respect there. They are not intimidating people, they're cool, both of them. Beyoncé's so sweet, and Jay is so focused.

'It wasn't as scary as Catherine Deneuve. That was my most terrifying screen kiss,' added Idris, who had starred alongside the French actress in *Belle Maman* in 1999. 'I was petrified. I mean, that woman is a legend.'

Obsessed tells the story of Lisa, an office temp – played by Ali Larter – who falls in love with her boss and attempts to seduce him by stalking him, drugging him and even attempting suicide in his bed.

Idris played the lead, the boss Derek Charles, and his wife Sharon was played by Beyoncé. Although there were many criticisms of the film's rather flimsy plot, it has been compared to *Fatal Attraction* and the final violent scene between Lisa and Sharon won the MTV Movie Award for Best Fight at the 2010 awards ceremony. Idris was nominated for the award for Outstanding Actor in a Motion Picture at the 41st NAACP Image Awards but lost out to Morgan Freeman's portrayal of Nelson Mandela in *Invictus*.

Not a man to stay down for long, Idris picked himself up, dusted himself off and moved straight into production for the crime film *Takers*. He played Gordon Jennings, the leader of a well-organised group of professional bank robbers pulled into one last job by a member of their gang recently released from jail. But a hard-boiled detective, played by Matt Dillon, is determined to interrupt their heist.

After the heist goes awry, Idris's character is shot in a tense three-way Mexican standoff, but he is rescued and the film ends with his line: 'Things are looking up,' although it is never made clear whether or not he survived his gun wounds.

It opened at Number One in the US Box Office, and Idris won the BET Award for Best Actor at the 2011 ceremony. He was also nominated for Best Supporting Actor in a Motion Picture at the NAACP Image Awards.

Riding high from the film's success, he flew to Scotland to start work on the low-budget psychological thriller *Legacy*. In this tiny independent film, he took on the role of Malcolm Gray, a former Special Forces veteran who was captured and tortured on a failed mission to Eastern Europe and later returned home to struggle with his paranoia, anxiety and a political conspiracy.

Looking for retribution, the black ops soldier takes refuge in a Brooklyn hotel room to brood over his past and the rise of his brother, a ruthless senator determined to stop at nothing to get into the White House.

Idris posted a picture of himself from the set on his new Twitter page, sparking a love affair with the social media site that would see him become one of the most popular actors, with almost a million followers.

Like Luther and Stringer Bell, two of his most iconic characters, Malcolm was a solitary, brooding type who preferred to keep people at arm's length.

Director Thomas Ikimi struggled to find funding for the film, however, and later apologised to the entire cast and crew for his bad mood throughout filming, due to the restrictions of the tight budget and the short shooting timetable. In fact, filming was only complete on the morning of the premiere in February 2010 and had to be shot entirely in Scotland, despite being based in Brooklyn. But, for Idris, the film was a huge breakthrough; although he realised the role would not prove as iconic as Stringer Bell, for him, the critical acclaim was more important than the box-office takings.

Idris, who was also an executive producer on the film, explained: 'It's a film that critically, in the festival world, has done really well, but, again, it's a tiny film and no one wants to write about it because no one really wants to support small-timey films.

'This character holes himself up in a room for a week, and in this room he starts to unravel who he is and where he's been. You start to understand that this is a man who's not very well.

And then you realise that you're not sure if some of the things we're seeing are real, and, in the end, there's a twist. I'm so proud of it, because we made it for no money.

'But I'm also proud of it because it actually does resonate for people who have someone like that in their family, someone who worked in the armed forces and the person that left and the soldier that came back are different.'

Although he felt the film was a giant step forward for his career, Idris never wants to be seen as predictable, and during this run of films, he had taken a break from his heavy roles to play Charles Miner in the American version of Ricky Gervais's hit TV comedy *The Office*. As vice president of northeast sales for Dunder Mifflin, Idris arrived as the company's new boss in Season Six. From the start, smooth and suave Charles was immediately popular with the staff, which made him a rival to bungling regional manager Michael Scott, played by Steve Carell.

For the first time, Idris had a chance to really tackle comedy head-on in some hilarious scenes with established comic actors, including the show's lead, Carell, who sparked off him. The first time their two characters meet, they seem to get along but this proves short-lived as Charles's no-nonsense management style soon clashes with Michael's more laid-back approach to office life. Charles is irritated by Michael's many attempts to impress him – which include cutting chunks out of bagels so they resemble a letter C, and ordering the staff to work extra hours without overtime pay. He then dissolves the party planning committee, set up by Michael to celebrate his 15 years with the company.

Charles Miner quickly becomes loathed by Michael, and Idris recalled Steve Carell once asked him: 'My character hates your character so much, it makes me want to hate you in real life. Is that OK?'

Humourless Charles also clashes with office prankster Jim, played by John Krasinski, keeping him under close scrutiny, although he attempts to please their new boss by feigning an interest in soccer. There is even an in-joke about Elba's most famous role at the time, when Michael admits he has been watching *The Wire* but doesn't understand a word of it.

Idris starred in six episodes, as well as the season finale, and became famous for announcing: 'I'm aware of the effect I have on women.'

Dabbling in comedy paid off for Idris, who went on to star in *The Big C*, a long-running US television show about a reserved suburban wife and mother who keeps her cancer a secret from the rest of her family and finds new friends to support her through her illness.

Laura Linney played Cathy, the high-school teacher diagnosed with terminal cancer, and Idris was cast as Lenny, a painter at the school who becomes her lover for a short period. But Cathy ends their brief affair as she re-examines her feelings for her husband Paul.

The show was hugely successful all over the world and led to Idris being nominated for a Primetime Emmy Award for Outstanding Guest Actor in a Comedy Series in 2011.

His relentless schedule of back-to-back filming continued in 2010 when he jetted down to Miami, Florida and Puerto Rico, to start work on *The Losers*, an action movie based on the adaptation of a comic book of the same name. Under the direction of Sylvain White, the film followed an elite black ops team of United States Special Forces operatives, known as The Losers, formed by Elba's character, ice-cold, knife-wielding Captain William Roque.

The team are sent to Bolivia in a search-and-destroy mission on a compound run by a drug lord. They end up stranded in

Bolivia and, when they realise they are to be executed, Roque steals a plane but, before he can escape, the plane is blown up by their enemies and he is killed. When filming wrapped in Puerto Rico, many fans agreed Idris had nailed another comic book adaptation and his big screen presence was growing fast.

Despite a loyal fan following for Idris, the film also received some terrible reviews, with critics calling it excessively violent and unoriginal, although the *New York Post* singled Idris out for praise, saying he 'deserved better'.

It may not have been the critical success he was looking for, but it led him directly to another comic book adaptation, which was to prove far more lucrative and exciting for the ambitious actor.

Thor, directed by Shakespearean actor Sir Kenneth Branagh, was based on the comic book character published by Marvel, and tells the story of a god who is exiled from his homeland of Asgard to Earth, but he must stop his brother Loki, who intends to become the new king of Asgard.

With a glittering cast including heavyweights such as Sir Anthony Hopkins and Natalie Portman, the film was destined for success. After receiving a personal call from Branagh, Idris knew he could hardly refuse his offer to cast him as Heimdall, the all-seeing, all-hearing gatekeeper of the Bifrost – the means of travelling between worlds.

Branagh said he was drawn to Idris's unique brand of sympathetic machismo, which he felt made him perfect to portray the kind of hero you can follow into battle – and can make a girl swoon! And the admiration was entirely mutual, for Idris later said it was the chance to work with Branagh that made the role impossible to turn down: 'Branagh called me up personally and said, "I know this isn't a big role, but I would really love to see you play it."

'It's Kenneth Branagh. I was like, "Definitely."'

The film was Elba's first foray into the high-tech world of 3D special effects.

'I did green screen for the first time,' he said afterwards. 'I wouldn't like to play a whole movie of green screen, though. You kind of forget the plot a little – like being in a Broadway play and doing it over and over and forgetting your line halfway through.'

It was also the first time he had been involved in a mega-budget blockbuster movie, and admitted he was stunned when he first saw huge billboards of himself in the street.

'It's odd,' he said. 'The *Thor* ones were humongous. I was in London and I saw me on the side of a bus, which was almost laughable, just this big face going past. I might ask to take one home – it's probably bigger than my mum and dad's house, but I'd like to see it in there.'

And the film itself was so much fun to shoot that Idris has even allowed himself to imagine having his own superhero franchise: 'I'd be lying if I said no,' he admitted. 'The dynamics of a superhero character are just larger. I've got a huge imagination, always had. I read *Spiderman* and *The Incredible Hulk* as a kid – and *The Beano*, naturally. So to imagine myself doing all that stuff is a real thrill.

'*Thor* is a huge, legendary comic book story and I wanted to be a part of it. Heimdall fighting the frost giants! It's just wicked.'

Actor Tom Hiddleston, who plays the villain Loki, said after working alongside him: 'Idris is truly a gentleman and an exceptionally diligent, creative man. He wears it all like a loose garment.'

'That's a wicked compliment,' Idris responded. 'But I guess I'm lucky. I have a bit of credibility that allows me moments when I'm working with geniuses in their field.'

Although Elba signed a hugely lucrative deal with Marvel Studios, committing him to four further feature films, his casting prompted a fierce debate among comic book fans, with some insisting it was wrong for a black man to play a Nordic god.

Idris himself dismissed the whole controversy as 'ridiculous'. He said: 'There has been a big debate about it: can a black man play a Nordic character?

'I was cast in *Thor* and I'm cast as a Nordic god. If you know anything about the Nords, they don't look like me but there you go. I think that's a sign of the times for the future. I think we will see multi-level casting. I think we will see that, and I think that's good.'

There was even a proposed boycott by the Council of Conservative Citizens, a group opposing inter-racial marriage and gay rights. They set up a website called boycott-thor.com to set out their opposition to what they saw as an example of left-wing social engineering.

'It [is] well known that Marvel is a company that advocates for left-wing ideologies and causes,' the site read. 'Marvel frontman Stan "Lee" Lieber boasts of being a major financier of left-wing political candidates. Marvel has viciously attacked the Tea Party movement, conservatives and European heritage. Now they have taken it one further, casting a black man as a Norse deity in their new movie *Thor*. Marvel has now inserted social engineering into European mythology.' The site chose to ignore its target's acting talents, referring to 'hip-hop DJ Elba' in apparent reference to the actor's career in East End nightclubs more than a decade earlier.

Addressing the casting issue, which he always finds tiresome, Idris pointed out: '*Thor* has a hammer that flies to him when he clicks his fingers. That's OK, but the colour of my skin is wrong?'

It is an issue that Idris has felt passionately about throughout his career, and he has never shied away from the debate surrounding the colour of his skin, however frustrating he might find it.

But he would prefer that the race issue should simply never arise at all: 'The less I talk about being black, the better,' he said recently.

Regardless of the controversy, he was thrilled to be joining the all-star cast of *Thor* to start shooting in the spring of 2010 at a specially constructed town in New Mexico. That summer, the film was heavily promoted at the San Diego Comic-Con International Festival, where exclusive clips were shown and subsequently released on the Internet, creating a huge buzz around the movie months before the official premiere.

'I'm really happy to be in it,' said Idris. 'I get to work with Anthony Hopkins – I love that.'

Inevitably, the film, when released in 3D amid a big-budget marketing blitz, was a massive box-office hit – taking $448.5 million worldwide. On top of that, the studio made vast fortunes from merchandise, DVD sales and soundtracks. Idris was nominated for a BET Award in the Best Actor category, and, although he lost out to Will Smith, within months work had started on the sequel.

CHAPTER NINE

BLOCKBUSTERS

Despite the phenomenal success of *Thor*, Idris suffered an unexpected setback when he was due to play the title character in a reboot of James Patterson's Alex Cross film franchise, but was suddenly replaced in February 2011 by his old adversary Tyler Perry. Though shocked to hit a bump in the road, when his career seemed to be going so smoothly, he dusted himself off and moved swiftly on to the next project he had in the pipeline.

He was to tackle another 3D superhero film based on the Marvel Comics anti-hero *Ghost Rider: Spirit of Vengeance*. Starring alongside Nicolas Cage, Idris was cast as Moreau, an alcoholic warrior monk, and was nominated for a BET Award for the role in 2011.

He admitted it was a new world for him, and many of his fans condemned Idris for choosing another box-office blockbuster, complaining that he had sold out to the Hollywood machine for a megabucks payday. But the actor was quick to defend himself: 'I get criticised for taking roles in films like *Ghost Rider* but, if you look at my résumé, I've mixed it up as much as I can,' he said.

Prometheus was Elba's next challenge, another science fiction epic, which was intended as a long-awaited prequel to the 1979 horror film *Alien*, although that link was very much downplayed when the movie was released in June 2012. Starring alongside Hollywood heavyweights including Charlize Theron, Michael Fassbender and Noomi Rapace, he appeared to have finally sealed his place on the A-list.

And he admitted that he was thrilled to be reunited with veteran director Ridley Scott at Pinewood Studios: 'I am ridiculously excited,' he said. 'I worked with Ridley on *American Gangster* and he is royalty to me. I was three years old when he first conceived the idea for *Alien*, but it's timeless.

'You look at the technology he was thinking about then: the robot characters, the mother ship. That shit has lived on in movies, on TV. But Ridley was the first to do it.'

He took on the role of Captain Janek and, although some critics blasted the film's convoluted plotline, Idris said: 'I've never had to explain *Prometheus* to people ever. Most people get it. I play Captain Janek, who is the captain of the ship basically, central to most storylines but not heavy in all storylines. Good part.

'Very much a working man. Everyone else in the film has sort of a scientific background or whatever. But my guy's an engineer. He's a pilot, flew war planes and now flies spaceships.'

While others wore space uniforms, Idris's character was seen in hooded sweatshirts: 'That's the idea,' he said. 'We want you to feel like you're looking at longshoremen or seamen that travel for long periods of time.

'The actual spaceship was built. Not in its entirety, but all its interiors are fully formed, built to scale, real size, functional. Ridley Scott wants the actors to feel as real as it can be.

'The green-screen acting was only outside of the windows, when I did the spaceship taking off and landing, that type of stuff. To be honest, it didn't affect me this much. In *Thor*, for example, when I was in that, there was a lot of green screen. You're literally talking to an actor with nothing around you.'

Idris admitted that he only took the part for the chance to work with director Ridley Scott again. They had first teamed up on *American Gangster* years earlier and he was eager to repeat the experience: 'I wanted to work with Ridley again,' he said. 'I loved working with him the first time. His return to this genre is a landmark in filmmaking.

'So to be a part of that certainly it feels like a big achievement for me. Ridley called me and said, "Look, this film isn't about Captain Janek at all. But I want a really good actor to play this part." So, he gave me the job and it was great.

'Biggest movie that I'm in, not biggest part.'

As soon as filming wrapped on *Prometheus*, Idris flew straight down to Atlanta to film *No Good Deed* (which is due for release in 2014) without a break. He was fascinated by his character: 'I'm playing a sexy, dangerous man in this film right now, though I don't find him sexy at all,' he admitted. 'I just find him depraved and horrible.

'But our goal is the audience has to like him even though they know he's done heinous shit. That's quite an interesting thing to play, actually.

'It's a thriller with Taraji P. Henson, an old-school thriller. I play a character that, well, without giving too much away, he basically breaks out of jail and then terrorises some people.

'I'm excited. Sam Miller, who directed the second instalment of *Luther*, he's directing it. It feels good. It's a good sort of slow-boil, old-school drama.

'I am executive producing it, yeah. I want to produce and

direct. This is one of the first exercises of me sort of bringing a team together to make something that I think will be good.'

As a result of his hectic back-to-back schedule, Idris was forced to miss two major events he was hoping to attend – the *Prometheus* premiere and the London Olympics in July 2012 – although he managed to squeeze in brief visits from his daughter.

'I'm not upset,' he said. 'It's just one of those things, the biggest film in the world and biggest event of the world and I can't be at either.

'I definitely wanted to be at the Olympics. It's in my neighbourhood where I grew up, in Hackney, and I've done some work with the Olympic team as an ambassador. So I certainly feel like I should be there.'

Idris was riding high, but he was not quite landing every role he went for. He missed out on a role he had hoped would bring him the chance to work with legendary director Quentin Tarantino. Although it was his convincing American accent that had won him the part of Stringer Bell in *The Wire*, it was apparently not good enough for Tarantino, who refused to cast him in his cowboy drama *Django Unchained*.

Once again, Idris was mired in controversy when news of Tarantino's decision emerged, with some commentators suggesting that it was in fact Idris who did not want to take part, having objected to the director's use of the word 'nigger' in some of his films.

'Tarantino and I had an 11-hour meeting,' Idris recalled. 'Eleven hours at his house chilling, talking about the film and talking about that character and I pretty much knew when I left that I wasn't going to be playing that part.'

Tarantino has been widely condemned for his portrayal of black characters and his movies are littered with expletives, including liberal use of the N-word. 'I've used that word in the past,' Idris went on. 'But it doesn't feel like a naturally good word to use. Because I'm African, and the origin of the word is deeper than just some throwaway word so really I tend not to use it now. Ever.'

Tarantino explained why he did not cast Idris, saying: 'Idris is British and this is an American story. I think a problem with a lot of movies that deal with this issue is they cast British actors to play the Southerners and it goes a long way to distancing the movie.

'They put on their gargoyle masks and they do their phoney accents and you are not telling an American story any more. They are just making hay of it, whether it be James Mason in *Mandingo* or Michael Caine in *Hurry Sundown*, they get British actors to do this.'

Idris himself was already sharply aware that his Englishness could count against him in America, where budding actors are hardly in short supply and there are more than enough established movie stars: 'Why do they need more actors? Why do they need more leading men?' he said. 'Every leading man – black, white, or other – is fighting for a handful of spots now. In fact, the tradition of the leading man is dying.

'That sort of handsome leading-man actor with a lifelong career because everyone adores him, audiences have moved on from that. They like more fresh faces.

'I'm not saying that's over completely, but it's definitely not as abundant as it was before. I feel like I come from a school of actors like, what's my man's name? Bradley Cooper. It's a school that's come from good ensemble acting and television backgrounds. It's just a longer process. They don't pop up in one movie and suddenly they're a superstar: Bradley's part of a franchise, *The Hangover*, which is bigger than him as a leading man.'

Idris has found himself repeatedly being asked about the issue of race in the movie industry, particularly after actor Samuel L. Jackson wrote a letter to the Oscars in 2011 demanding to know why there were no black presenters.

Idris said: 'Opportunities are not the same. It's just boring now. It's true. There's no such thing as a black actor or a white actor. We're just actors.

'Are there differences between black actor's opportunities? Yes, there are. It's been said.

'Let the work do the talking. For a younger actor that is black and reading this article, I'd rather him hear about the success than about how tough it was. I just feel like we've had those moments, hugely.

'Anyway, everyone's going to be brown one way or another. It's true. It's just a fact. It's the way the human race is going. Everyone's going to be brown. The term "brown" means there's so many different cultures mixing now. Luther, Stringer Bell, being awarded jobs where the character was neither black nor white – those are success stories to me. Stringer Bell is a drug dealer.

'I have more white fans of Stringer than I have black fans. You know what I mean? It has nothing to do with the fact that he's black at all. It wasn't that Stringer was black or white that made him attractive or appealing, it was his situation and the way he dealt with that.

'If anything, the whole *Wire* clan was more reminiscent of a classic Italian gangster family than it was what we see in the stereotypical drug family.

'I get these roles because I can act and that's it. Hopefully that's it. I think the less I talk about being black, so to speak, the better.'

Despite the deeply divisive nature of the debate that sparked passionate opinions on all sides, it appeared to do Idris no harm as he continued to land bigger and better roles. After filming wrapped on *Prometheus*, one of 2012's most eagerly anticipated blockbusters, he reprised his role as the imposing Heimdall in the superhero sequel *Thor: The Dark World*, and went on to beat Hollywood heavyweight Tom Cruise to play an inspiring leader and tough robot called General Stacker Pentecost in the monster-infested blockbuster *Pacific Rim*.

Although originally created with Cruise in mind, Mexican filmmaker Guillermo del Toro, who directed the film, leapt at the chance to cast Idris in the role instead.

'It was a part you just could not turn down,' said Idris, who admits he was left stunned when Hollywood royalty was cast aside to make way for him.

'Here I am in a job that should have been his,' he said, when asked about being chosen over Tom Cruise. 'I was a bit embarrassed. This is a true story, Guillermo called me and said, "Tom Cruise doesn't want to do it so I want you!" I said, "OK, thanks, Tom." He has a huge sense of humour but it was a coveted role and I'm sure Tom would have loved to have done it, they could have tried to work it out or whatever, but the fact that here's a role that could have gone to Tom Cruise, and here I am, it does add a certain sort of responsibility almost, you know?

'Most actors don't get to choose their roles, you get a job, you work it and you move on, but as I sort of climb the ladder a bit I get to choose roles. So now the films that I am leaning towards have something to say.

'If I'm going to spend two and a half hours, or even an hour, watching a film, I want a message from it. So this film, even though it's a huge sci-fi movie, it does have a really great human story.'

And del Toro was absolutely delighted with his choice of casting, and has said of his leading man: 'He exudes power but he doesn't exude the power of The Man, of the Establishment, he doesn't have the authority that belongs to a group. It's an authority that belongs exclusively to him.'

Idris relished his role at the heart of the loud effects-driven blockbuster, and, while many actors like to pretend special effects movies are meaningful works of art akin to Shakespeare, he accepts it for what it is: 'It's a completely different animal to working on something like *Luther*,' he admitted. 'With that series, we run with the raw emotion so much more. With something like *Pacific Rim*, it's a little bit more manufactured.'

The immense monster-versus-robot fight was the action film of the summer when released in 2013, but, with a staggering budget of $190 million, it was also a huge investment in Elba's ability to hold the world's sympathy as a military commander who faces down an invasion of monsters from beneath the sea by roaring the infamous words: 'Today we are cancelling the apocalypse!'

Del Toro said there were only a handful of actors he could possibly consider for the powerful 'Apocalypse' speech and, even after narrowing it down to four, he always wanted Idris because he says he appears uncomfortable with the job: 'Idris, when he's acting, I don't think he's content,' said the director. 'He's very social but he has boundaries.'

Of course, Elba had made huge movies before – *Prometheus* and *Thor*, for example – but this was the first time he had really shouldered a blockbuster and he was enthusiastic about being at the heart of the machine. When the film was ready for release, he embarked on a publicity tornado, hopping between chat show sofas across the globe.

'When you're in a movie like this, the gear up for the release is completely different to what I'm used to,' he explained.

But del Toro, like *The Wire* producer David Simon, admitted he had been shocked when he heard the news that Idris was actually an Englishman, and that, for Idris, was the greatest vindication of his abilities as an actor.

Del Toro, however, saw much more in Idris than just his convincing American accent: 'Rodin sculptures have these oversized hands and they seem incredibly weighted by their own humanity,' he said. 'Idris is sort of like that. He's over human. And he has the most amazing eyes. Some actors have the gift of empathy with the audience. And it is a gift – it's not technique or training. There are just actors you care for.'

Despite the director's enthusiasm, there was yet again a certain level of criticism about casting a black man at the centre of a science fiction movie, something that enraged Idris, since he was forced to deal with the race issue once more: 'If you're thinking in the middle of the movie, "Oh he's black and in sci-fi", you're not watching the same movie as me.'

Regardless of the hype, he has managed to stay down to earth. Asked if he would study the legendary director's way of working while on the set of *Pacific Rim*, he said: 'Sometimes. But you get the same satisfaction by getting to know the crew. I realise that I find myself really attracted to crews, and I get to know them because they are the ones who are doing the work. The directors are only telling them what to do, so for me getting to understand who my crew is helps me get one step closer.

'From Guillermo, I learned how to make a big film. In television, you come in, there are two cameras maybe; you set up a nice wide shot. In *Luther*, we spend time making sure a shot is a *Luther* shot. But with Guillermo, when he stepped on the set and I learned what it is to do big "pushes" [filming techniques] as you say your line and "sweeps" with the camera, it is quite impressive.

'I remember doing this massive rain scene in which I am

watching this Jaeger fall out of the sky and it was quite fun. It was a massive stage built at the top of this roof. It felt so real.

'*Pan's Labyrinth* is my favourite of his films, because it is just beautifully shot and delicately made. It is that way he blends a war film with a fantasy. Amazing.'

Idris relished the chance to constantly learn about the craft of filmmaking while on the set: 'Well, Guillermo del Toro's film is much more an Earth/human story with the looming attack of another race,' he explained. 'Very different. Guillermo del Toro is an amazing director to work with. I learned so much about precision from him – about looking at you now and then looking one layer behind you at the leaves, and then looking at the wall behind you and then looking at shadows on the wall.

'My depth of field is now so unbelievably clear I feel like I want to direct now because of what Guillermo taught me. His attention to detail is amazing; his attention to sort of how to manipulate the audience to keep driving them forward in the story. As an actor, you kind of say the words, but he wanted us to really connect to each emotion.

'Whether the last time you saw me on the screen was six minutes ago or not, there was a real sort of connection to each one any time you were seeing me. That's not something you teach, but it's something that I was aware that he was paying attention to. It was interesting.

'My character is yet another man of authority but this time much higher up. He's the head of the army and the army is the essential fighting force against these monsters. The world is crumbled and this alien lived underneath the surface of the Earth for a long time. Our only defence has been these massive robots that fight back – they're basically tanks that are put together to look like men and can walk.

'I play the leader of that sort of movement. Then we lose our funding, basically, and the world decides to build walls around countries, which basically means the rich can get in and the poor can't.

'So our characters go, "No. We're going to fight this our way." It could be a box-standard, fight-against-the-aliens sort of film, but not with Guillermo.

'It's certainly a commentary on if the world were under attack who would survive and who wouldn't. Interestingly enough, the poor would probably more survive than the rich because they have less and are used to less; therefore, more resilient and more tough.

'If an alien attacks a big skyscraper, people in the skyscraper are going to die. The people on the floor may not.'

Above left: Idris Elba and guest attend *GQ Magazine*'s 2004 Men of the Year event in Los Angeles.

Above right: 'Daddy's Little Girl': pictured with his daughter Isan in 2007.

Below left: Idris and his co-star in *The Wire*, Dominic West, attend the BAFTA Television Awards, 2009.

Below right: As Charles Miner in NBC's *The Office* in 2009.

Above: Idris Elba and Jamie Foxx attend the 'Pre' Party in celebration of the BET Awards in 2009.

Below: DJ Big Driis: Idris performs as his alter ego (*left*) at Lincoln After Dark in New Orleans in 2009 and (*right*) at Cowarth Park Polo Club in Ascot, England in 2013.

Above: Alongside Nelson Mandela's second wife Winnie at the premiere of
Mandela: Long Walk to Freedom in Johannesburg, 2013.

Below: (*l to r*) Tinie Tempah, Laura Whitmore, Idris Elba, Damian Lewis, Helen
McCrory, Victoria Pendleton, Sam Claflin and Kate Adie pose for a photograph
with Prince Charles at the Prince's Trust & Samsung Celebrate Success Awards
in London in 2013.

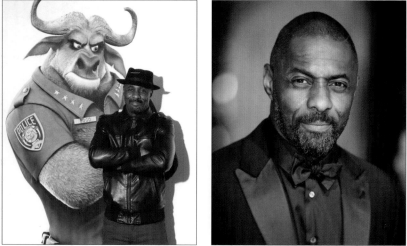

Above: Idris puts his new gong for 'Best Male Lead' to the test at the 2016 Film Independent Spirit Awards. Pictured next to him is Cary Fukunaga, director of *Beasts of No Nation*, and Idris's young co-star for the same film, Abraham Attah.

Below left: Uncanny likeness: Idris poses next to his character, Chief Bogo, at the UK Gala Screening of *Zootropolis* at London's Hackney Picturehouse.

Below right: When scrubbed up, few would dispute that Idris looks the part for the much-vaunted role of the next James Bond – a topic which has both excited and plagued him in recent times.

All photographs © Getty Images

CHAPTER TEN

DETECTIVE LUTHER

Idris was settling into a new way of life in Hollywood, as a bona fide star, and his roles on the silver screen were gradually growing in stature – meaning he was finally in a position to turn down more jobs than he accepted. But he had not forgotten where he came from, and he knew that he could not turn down a unique opportunity to play the lead in a top-quality BBC drama, back home in Britain, when it came his way in 2010.

'Yeah, "Stringer" Bell opened up a lot of doors for me in America, but before that in England my doors were opened 10 years prior in smaller TV roles,' he explained. 'I remember being at the pinnacle of my career in England and then going to America and losing it, but then coming back with "Stringer" Bell and regaining it. It's just peaks and troughs.'

He may have risen through the ranks to become one of the biggest British stars in America, but, when he was offered the role of Detective Chief Inspector John Luther, the East End boy returned to his roots to tackle something fresh and completely different from the movies he had been appearing in.

A decade after he had moved to the States to advance his acting career, he wanted to star in a quality drama series that would resonate with his parents, and could be watched by his auntie Mae in Peckham, who had yet to see any of his work!

Luther was to become the most eagerly anticipated psychological crime drama in years, starring Idris in the title role. It was a major upheaval for him to leave his new girlfriend, aspiring model and dancer, Desiree Newberry, who had just given birth to their son in Miami (more of which later), to film in London for six months, but he knew the project would be a hit and he was right. The first series of six episodes, which was broadcast in May 2010, was immediately followed by a second, and BBC controller Danny Cohen was quick to announce news of a third series.

Idris explained at the time why he felt that he simply could not turn down the job: 'Here I am, a boy that grew up with the BBC and ITV, then Channel 4. If you had a show on BBC1 where you were the lead man, you had made it.

'And here I am – all the movie roles in the world could not top being offered *Luther*. How could you not take that?'

Although many people were surprised when Idris packed his bags and left the States to film a television series back in the UK – something he was strongly advised against by his management – for him, it was a carefully considered career move.

'*Luther* came to me and I was doing well,' he recalled. 'Some members of my team at the time thought it seemed like a lateral step. But most actors in England realise that the pinnacle of your career over here is to work for the BBC, on a show where you're the lead.

'So I thought it was a step forward – and it has been. For one thing, it's the only performance of mine that ever got me a Golden Globe nomination.'

Elba's character, who heads up the Metropolitan Police's Serious Crime Unit, is a dedicated police officer but also a genius. He suffers a mental breakdown after a traumatic case involving a child killer, which leads him down dark paths to catch other criminals. Obsessive and possessed, he is sometimes dangerous in the violence of his fixations. And the price he pays for his dedication is a heavy one: he is unable to stop himself from becoming consumed by the darkness of the crimes he tries to solve.

For Luther, the job always comes first, he will stop at nothing to bring criminals to justice – at the expense of all other relationships in his life, including his tense romance with mysterious murder suspect Alice Morgan, played by Ruth Wilson.

Idris takes the archetypal moody cop and somehow makes him edgier, so the audience are often not quite sure if DCI Luther is on the side of the good or the bad, and he has found himself under suspicion from even his closest aides.

The drama is gripping, and Idris fills the screen with brooding intensity.

'He's a slightly fantastic character based on the fact that coppers these days are not built that way,' Idris explained. 'Coppers follow procedure or the media has a feeding frenzy. So Luther is sort of like a superman because he gets away with stuff.'

An aspect that particularly appealed to Idris was that no issue was made of the character's race in the script. 'We haven't seen a Luther before,' he said. 'Not in England. Even in America, black men in leading roles are few and far between. But it's great it's never, ever mentioned in our show – I adore that.

'And that, I tell you, that is an achievement. But it will be drawn upon, of course it will. In England, we're a little more modern in the sense integration is no big news for us, know what I mean? Been there, done that.

'My generation, we're all integrated, musically, culturally. We went to the same schools, we all got the same education; we all had the same leaders. With Luther, yes, he's a black lead, and, yes, it's a first. But still. If Luther is refreshing because he's a nigger that don't give a fuck, then OK! But he's still a detective. Who cares if he's black?'

Creator Neil Cross has told how famous detectives such as Sherlock Holmes influenced him when he wrote how Luther applies his great intellect to solving crimes. The Booker Prize-nominated author was also inspired by the format of American TV detective series *Columbo*, in which the audience is aware of the identity of the criminal but not how they will be caught – as opposed to the conventional format of the audience discovering the criminals at the same time as the characters do.

When Cross conceived a character who was perpetually suicidal, with a sprinkling of intuitive genius, almost off the bleak end of the maverick cop spectrum, he never dared dream Idris would take on the role. 'He's a feral Columbo and a bookish Dirty Harry fighting in a sack,' said Cross. 'I didn't write the part with Idris in mind, because, well, because he's Idris Elba.

'We talked a lot about how perfect he'd be, but as far as I was concerned this was an entirely hypothetical conversation – the world's full of writers and producers talking about how perfect Idris Elba would be for their project.

'So I didn't consider him a serious possibility. Perhaps because the BBC didn't want to freak me out, I didn't actually know the script had been sent to him until he'd read and liked it. Finding this out, I have to say, was a pretty big moment.'

Despite the writer's doubts, Idris was hooked as soon as he saw the first script: 'I've played bad guys, and I've played good guys,' he said. 'But Luther is a real character study. He straddles the fence between being a copper who follows procedure, and being a bad-tempered vigilante.

'Now, could he really exist? Maybe there could be a senior black detective in London, but I did the research and there weren't too many of them. Luther is larger than life; he's almost a superhero.'

Over the course of three action-packed series, Luther has seen his beloved estranged wife murdered by his best friend and contemplated suicide. He found new love, but of course that was not enough to make him happy.

'He's trying to make a human connection, which is rare for him,' explained Idris, who admits that he would become so absorbed in the role during filming that he, like his alter ego, is not very nice to be around.

'People steer clear of me when I'm making it,' he said. 'It isn't that I'm unfriendly, but I get into the dark zone that John Luther occupies, and have to stay there.'

Cross always hoped that somehow Elba would be persuaded to agree to play the lead despite the fame he had found in America, thanks to *The Wire*: 'He had a peculiar mixture of fantastic luck and terrible luck in that he found what every actor dreams of and fears, which is the life-defining role,' said Cross, adding that *The Wire* only became a cult hit after Idris's character had been dramatically killed off. 'Stringer was already dead when the rest of the world fell in love with him. To have what seemed at the time to be a career-defining role – and it was already over by the time it became career defining.'

As he prepared to start filming the third series, Idris explained: 'Well, we're going back to a four-episode format, high-octane *Luther* stuff. We're going to close out a couple of storylines. We're really preparing for the big-screen *Luther*. It's a goal, a very strong goal. It's not in stone yet, but it's something we definitely want to aim towards.'

He was concerned that the third series would not be as successful as the previous two had been, but of course he needn't have worried: 'We haven't been on TV for almost a year and a bit,' he recalled when it aired. 'I was very nervous at the time, thinking, "Oh, I am not sure that the audience is going to go with it," but it did. The first episode of the new series got between five and seven million viewers.

'It was on a Tuesday. There was nothing else on, mind you, but it was great. We got a great response and it trended on Twitter for at least an hour.'

Although critically acclaimed in Britain, in terms of audience numbers, the show fared much better when it crossed the Atlantic. *The Hollywood Reporter* raved: 'Strong writing and a fine cast, especially *The Wire*'s Idris Elba as the title character, make this grim export from Britain a compelling, intelligent cop show.'

It became BBC America's top-rated show, gaining the network its highest-ever quarterly ratings and Idris was nominated for a Golden Globe in 2011. He missed out that year, and the award was won by Al Pacino for *You Don't Know Jack*, but, at the 69th Golden Globe Awards in January 2012, he won Best Actor in a Series, Mini-Series or Motion Picture Made for Television.

Accepting this award, he said: 'This is for the fans. I have the most loyal fans in the world, all over the world and I appreciate it. I want to thank Neil Cross, who is phenomenal and changed my life.'

He then dedicated the win to 'My beautiful daughter Isan, who's at home having a Golden Globe party'. 'We did it, Mama, I love you,' he said.

Winning the Golden Globe changed the quality of the parts Elba was being offered almost overnight: 'Prior to *Luther*, I was doing sort of like drop-in film work: *Obsessed*, *Takers*, *This Christmas*

– films that were sort of more in a space that was skew
if you like, and smaller films. Good parts, but smaller,'
'*Luther* gave me an opportunity to show that I love to act. I
character actor in my heart of hearts. So, *Luther* gave me not only
a confidence but a showcase to kind of go, "Oh yeah, that's right,
I do make up these other characters and can act".

'Plus, it changed the kind of people that were calling. I got
Pacific Rim because Guillermo del Toro loved the show. Ridley
Scott saw me again in *Luther* and was like, "Oh my God, I
promised Idris he and I would work together again." Because
he did, and then we did.'

The angry, anti-Establishment detective, caught the attention
of key industry players across the globe. Distinguished directors
got in touch as soon as they had finished watching.

'No one expected it to be as successful as it was. It was a
massive risk,' Idris admitted.

Elba was also nominated for a Primetime Emmy Award for
the role in 2011 and 2012, and won a BET Award for *Luther*
in 2010. He also won a Black Reel Award for the role the same
year, and in 2011 he won the Outstanding Actor category at the
Image Awards. But the greatest accolade for Idris personally
was when he came to the attention of scores of Hollywood
hotshots, including the producer of the crime drama
Elementary, a modern interpretation of the Sherlock Holmes
stories, which stars fellow British actor Jonny Lee Miller.

'My wish list?' said producer Rob Doherty at the Television
Critics Association Winter Tour. 'I love Idris Elba. I'm a big fan
of *Luther*, he's amazing.'

Unfortunately, Idris's mother Eve was not so enthusiastic,
even though she finally had a chance to watch her son on
British television: 'It's great being on HBO in America but my
mum just wanted me to be in *EastEnders*. This was the closest

said. 'I've done more roles in other
al accent, so it was an amazing
Luther, an English character, with my
itish TV.'

ere so loyal to *Luther* because of the
script, and the fact that they never
des or patronised the viewer in any
way. we ...... introduction element. There was no
spoon-feeding or placating where it was like, "We're not sure
what we are but you can help us determine that."

'What we realised was that the audience really responded to
the unorthodox darkness of it, which is unlike the BBC. We
wanted a *film noir* element and a larger-than-life Gotham City
feel. London's a big character in *Luther* and we wanted it to
look like this monster.'

Idris became heavily involved and even took on the task of
producing the show, as well as starring in it: 'I love to act but I
also love the logistics of pulling it together, and watching great
filmmakers and actors making it happen,' he explained. 'I'd like
to direct more than produce, but being a producer is quite a
satisfying thing.'

He is often asked to compare Luther with his other famous
character, Stringer Bell. Explaining the differences, he said: 'I
think, with Stringer, I brought an English sensibility to an
American character, and, with Luther, I bring American
sensibilities to an English character.

'Stringer, on the page, he read like the *consigliere*, the man
next to the man. But I sophisticated Stringer up with how subtle
he was.

'Luther – he's way bigger in his reactions than an English cop
would ever be. He's very American-esque in that way.

'I think part of the TV show's popularity in England is that it's sort of ridiculous to see an Englishman that big in a lot of these scenes. But it actually works because of how grandiose some of the crimes are.

'I think Luther had some sort of trauma. The thing about being traumatised, if you're a size 12 and you traumatise your shoes, when you put your shoes back on, they're probably bigger than the last time you wore them. I think that's what happened with Luther. I think he just didn't come back to his ground zero after some really traumatic things in his life.

'It's bigger than life; it's like a movie. The character is big. He is not your typical English gent but yet he is. He goes after horrible, horrible people and we are fascinated as audiences watching him and observing him.

'And then you have got a cop that's equally as horrible when he goes after you. That is what its appeal is. I became a producer later on and my role is really just keeping the integrity of the character and also the show.

'I protect the "Lutherisms". They range from everything like the type of actors that come into the show, the type of camera-work. "That doesn't feel very *Luther* but this does" – I say that quite a bit.'

Idris was rightly proud of all he had accomplished as part of the strong BBC production team. 'There's a huge sense of achievement with it,' he said. 'You've got to understand that I'm still an actor and being offered parts that are challenging, motivating and iconic is the greatest buzz. But being able to say that I'm part of the team that put it together and helps keep its integrity alive is exciting in a different way. I love that.'

Indeed, he would become so absorbed in the character that he would even talk about himself in the third person: 'When I'm playing Luther, Idris ends up in a darker place,' he admitted.

But Idris was shocked when some people questioned the

violence in the show and raised the issue of his being a poor black role model: 'If anyone really was to tell me they worried about that after actually watching *Luther*, I'd be surprised,' he declared.

'In what part of that show should I have been representing black culture a bit more? It's a big, fantastical thrill show about evil. I mean, it's not like the show is close to reality.'

He has a point about some of the more far-fetched storylines. The first series ended when his character tracked down his best friend – who had just murdered Luther's wife and was trying to frame him for it – with the help of the strange friendship he had forged with serial killer Alice.

Series two saw Luther suicidal and on the hunt for killer twins, while series three started with a serial killer who dressed his victims like rock singer Siouxsie Sioux.

Luther had also found love with a beautiful vintage shop owner called Mary Day, played by Sienna Guillory, but, after years of beating up, shooting and threatening suspects, his bosses at the Met started to mount an internal investigation into his unconventional methods. 'We're saying if you live life the way he does there will inevitably be consequences – and our intention is to show that,' Idris explained. 'I mean, we stay within the realms of the fantastical – that's what *Luther* is. A mad, violent Scotsman conducts the investigation.

'But it's a way of showing that we're paying attention – that detectives like this in the force often will be investigated. This is the reality – as close to reality as you'd expect from *Luther*.

'He makes an attempt at love, at human connection, which is rare for him.

'In the previous season, he was trying to kill himself. He's moved on from there now. I mean, he's even had a haircut – he's looking like a proper policeman. I hope that's not going to alienate people.'

On the overall theme of the third season, Idris explained: 'Internally, we wanted to get closer to Luther and not follow a route of him getting more and more depressed, taking drugs and wanting to shoot himself.

'We wanted to get to know him a little bit better and find out what he would do under pressure. Understanding the legacy of everything he's lived with, how do we get into that? Having him investigated was the ultimate autopsy on him.

'And we wanted to make that stretch over the season, so that at the end, when we say the last words, "Now what?", we wanted the audience to say, "Now what?", and literally look at Luther and go, "I don't know where you can go from here, pal."

'We wanted to really look at the weight of his actions and how that's changed him, or not changed him. At the same time, we want to really keep our audience thrilled. Our bad guys in *Luther* are always vivid and horrible, but we wanted to enhance that this season, elevating it in a darker way. That was the theme we wanted to explore.'

As for his character's transformation over the three seasons, Idris explained: 'In Season One, Luther was coming out of the end of a very weird, dark time. It was stuff that we didn't really explore, but post-traumatic stuff happened. He was willing to kill someone, practically, in the first season, in order to get to the truth.

'By Season Three, I think he's stabilised himself somewhat, even though he's gone through such trauma. He's managed to stabilise himself, so that he doesn't get to that place as quickly and as recklessly. There's been a massive change for him. I wouldn't say he's grown up, but he's definitely started to grasp onto the idea that he just can't get away with the way he is living. That's a big, massive arc.

'And we see Luther smiling, not from irony, but from actual happiness, a couple of times.'

Unfortunately for *Luther*'s legion of fans, Idris has been too busy working on blockbusters in Hollywood to commit to making a fourth series. But the good news is that he still dreams of turning *Luther* into a feature film, and, although he has been too committed recently to finalise discussions for the project, these days he certainly has the clout to get it made.

'There's talk,' he said in 2013. 'The audience was very, very loyal to us. Creator Neil Cross and I want to take it to the cinema. If there's another season of it, that won't be the final chapter – that [the final chapter] will be a reincarnation of *Luther* as a film.

'That is definitely on the cards, we've been really lucky that *Luther* is so popular. It's a small show, we did four episodes and we got such a massive following worldwide so Neil Cross and I are aiming to do the film.

'I'm speaking to him and we're trying to pull it together. It's an ambitious project because it's a television show but we suspect that it's going to be as successful on TV and on film as well.'

Cross is ready and waiting for Idris to find a long enough gap in his schedule to start shooting: 'I've written the script and we hope to get the film made,' said the show's creator, who has also written a *Luther* novel and is working on a second. 'Idris is a brilliant leading man and we've hoped to turn *Luther* into a movie for a long time. It will follow his career in the earlier days, when he is still married to Zoe, and the final scene in the film is the first of the initial TV series.'

The prequel would also restore Luther's sidekick DS Justin Ripley, played by Warren Brown, to life, as well as his shamed colleague DCI Ian Reed, played by Steven Mackintosh. His slain wife Zoe, played by Indira Varma, would also return.

Idris is equally keen: 'That's where the ultimate *Luther* story will unfold, is on the big silver screen,' he said. 'London as a huge backdrop and a very menacing, horrible character to play against.

'When I started *Luther*, I'd reached a point in my career when it was perfect for me,' he continued. 'Coming back to it was a bit of a choice and I got to be producer. I wanted to make sure it was as good as ever.'

There were nearly two years between Series Two and Three because Idris was too busy in Hollywood to fit it in. And, although he would not exactly spell it out, now he has become almost too famous for the series, although he says he would also relish another chance to film on the familiar territory of his childhood: 'We made a lot of the last series in the same East London streets I used to run around in,' he says. 'My parents still live there, and my core group of mates, people I've known for 25 years or more.'

Despite his move across the Atlantic, Idris has always remained loyal to the BBC and has been quick to defend British drama, even when it was criticised by his former cast mate from *The Wire*, Dominic West: 'I suppose for someone who has made a lot of money out of being in an American TV show I shouldn't moan but it does annoy me when Beatrix Potter is made by a Texan.'

'The BBC has taken a leap of faith in the idea that its history could dictate what it does next,' said Idris. 'It stopped following everybody else's history or anyone else's trends. The BBC is world renowned for making great dramas, so what it's done is said, "Oh you know what? Of course we're good at making drama. We'll do what we do best."

'Hiring great writers, performers and directors is part of its legacy, and I sort of fit into that, I guess.'

He also believes that powerful dramas such as *Luther* have only benefited from the onslaught of 'structured reality' TV shows like *The Only Way Is Essex*.

'They're already starting to wear out,' he said. 'It's a genre that'll eat itself. But what it's actually done is train viewers to crave great actors, great writing and great performances. They want to see that. You think, "If I want train wreck television, I'll watch a reality show. If I want drama and heightened performance, then I'll watch that."

'I've watched *Jersey Shore* and [MTV UK's] *Geordie Shore* and compared the two. *Geordie Shore* is about kids from Newcastle. It's very similar to *Jersey Shore* but raunchier.'

Despite being a secret fan of reality television, Idris has turned down dozens of offers to appear on any such shows. He once revealed that he is a skilled tap dancer, but has no plans ever to appear on *Dancing With the Stars*.

'No. There it is,' he says. 'It's a guilty pleasure to watch it.'

Idris's meaty role in *Luther* won him many famous fans, including Rolling Stone Ronnie Wood: 'What? No fucking way! Are you serious? Fucking hell!' was his reaction on hearing about Wood.

Notoriously frosty American *Vogue* editor-in-chief Anna Wintour also revealed that she was among the show's huge fan base: 'Anna is a fan of *Luther*,' said Idris. 'We just built up a rapport on emails.'

His surprising admirer even helped him out with fashion advice for his directorial debut, *Pavement Psychologist*, a film he made in May 2013 for the Sky Arts channel about an accountant obsessed with shoes, played by Anna Friel, whose life is thrown into turmoil when she encounters a homeless man.

'I told her [Wintour] about my plan for the movie and she just said, "Darling, you have to get the right shoes." And then she sent me a list of shoes. Why not?'

Idris wrote the script for *Pavement Psychologist* while he was in South Africa, filming *Mandela: Long Walk to Freedom*, and having to undergo hours in the make-up chair every morning to be transformed into the iconic statesman. 'My iPad was clamped in front of me and that's how I wrote it,' he recalled, holding his hands up to an imaginary keyboard in the air.

'Interesting thing about scriptwriting is that you've got this software that does all the work, the formatting, so then you're like, "I can make these people say whatever the fuck I want!"

'It was like a God complex, it was amazing.'

Friel agreed that Elba's enthusiasm was infectious, claiming he called her from the make-up chair, having just landed in South Africa, and then shot the drama over his 40th birthday, without any break. And he proved as tough on his cast as he is on himself: 'He made me walk around Croydon for 14 hours in the tiniest torture shoes,' laughed the actress. 'But he's not someone you want to have a whinge around.'

'Anna's so funny,' Idris smiled. 'She said, "It's a good script, but why feet?" I had to be honest with her. There came a moment right there where the actor was looking at me and saying, "Why did you write this story?" And I had to say, "Well, I've got a fucking fetish for feet."

'I spilled the beans, told the truth about it. I know how it developed and when, and I've never articulated it and it just seeped into that script. 'She was like, "Wow, that's weird." And I said, "I know!"

'But this is the kind of filmmaker I'm going to be. I'm going to write about stuff that's happened to me, or that I've wanted to happen or that I think about deeply.

'And I loved writing; it really lit a fire. I swear to God, man, if I wrote a one-man show or film, I'd write the fucking wickedest dialogue for myself: all the things I'd wanted to say in a movie.'

Although Luther was not created as a black character, the show was heralded as a trail-blazer on both sides of the Atlantic because it was the first British cop show ever to have a black actor as a lead.

'My skin colour wasn't a big issue either way,' said Idris, who would much rather people talked about his talent as an actor or his performance in the role. 'I might be seen as some sort of beacon but I really don't want to be pigeonholed as a black actor. I've shot myself in the foot a few times speaking about black actors; I'm over it. I don't know what a black actor is now – I think we're becoming colour blind.'

However, the issue of black actors having to move to America to find decent roles still haunted him. Despite his attempts at playing it down, acclaimed Shakespearean actor David Harewood then stated that watching Idris play Luther proved to him that in order to get an 'authoritative role' he needed to follow in his footsteps and also make the move to America. It paid off for Harewood too, who is now best known for playing CIA deputy director David Estes in the hit double-agent drama *Homeland*. 'It took Idris a long time to crack it but now he can come back and he's a national treasure,' said Harewood. 'For me, that's what I knew I needed to do because I simply wouldn't have been given a role of weight or authority here in the UK. That's just a fact.'

Regardless of the race debate, Idris remains justly proud of *Luther*: 'The biggest risk was making me the lead actor; even though I was from a popular American show; British audiences hadn't seen much of me for 10 years.

'So I'm surprised at how popular it's become all over the world, and in America in particular, where they're really embracing it. It's got brilliant writing and I think what appeals to people abroad is it's not your typically British stiff-upper-lip stuff; you're seeing a six-foot-something guy kicking ass and they like it.

'That's certainly what they seem to get excited about.'

CHAPTER ELEVEN

HEARTBREAK

Professionally, life was heading in the right direction for Idris but he has certainly suffered his fair share of heartbreak along the way. As well as his ill-fated marriage to make-up artist Hanne Norgaard, which fell apart when they moved to New York, he also had another secret whirlwind romance, which he prefers not to talk about.

His second, previously unknown, wedding was registered in Las Vegas in 2006. Local records reveal that one Idris Akuna Elba married Sonya Nicole Hamlin, who is believed to be a lawyer. The marriage did not last, however.

Just 24 hours later the couple had their wedding annulled.

Indeed, Elba's spokeswoman Michelle Benson has confirmed that the marriage was 'annulled after a day', dismissing it simply as a 'Vegas wedding'.

But Idris is a charmer and he bounced back pretty quickly. Picking up the pieces of his broken heart, he flew off to visit his ex-wife and their daughter in Atlanta, where he happened to find himself passing the time in a nightclub called Magic City, where one of the scantily clad professional dancers immediately caught his eye.

Desiree Newberry, an aspiring fashion model, was working as a pole dancer in the club and their romance quickly heated up. He and Desiree had been dating for a couple of years and their relationship was going well when she fell pregnant. Idris could not have been happier: he had quickly fallen in love with the stunning model, who by then had landed herself several magazine covers, and they had started living together in Miami. Whenever he had a break between filming commitments, besotted Idris would fly down to Florida to spend whatever time he had with his girlfriend in the Miami beach house he had bought for them.

His work often kept them apart but, when Desiree gave birth to their son, Idris was overjoyed. Although he never revealed the boy's name, for a while, he admitted later, it was among the happiest times of his life. The baby was born just as he was starting work on *Luther* and he told how he felt on top of the world. 'The celebration of having a son – from a man's perspective, it's massive,' he said.

Of course, when the baby was born, Idris happily announced the news to his friends and family, even to reporters when he was promoting *Luther* and various other films. During interviews for his film *The Loser* in 2010, he excitedly told a writer from *The New York Times* that he had a son. And, for the first time, he felt like he had it all.

But, when he returned to Desiree and their baby in Miami, after filming *Luther* in London in 2010, a crushing heartbreak lay in store for him. He was stunned to discover that the son he thought he had fathered with Desiree was not, in fact, his child after all. And it was only after spending years dealing with the shock that Idris felt able to actually discuss the bitter betrayal he felt.

At first, he refused to explain the mystery, but it later emerged that a few months after the boy was born it had been suggested to him, not from the child's mother, but from elsewhere, that everything was not as it seemed.

'It wasn't immediately obvious,' he recalled. 'Well, it was, because he did not look like me. But it wasn't immediately obvious what had gone down.'

Eventually, Desiree agreed to let Idris take a paternity test and his worst fears were confirmed when it was revealed that he was not the baby's natural father. A year later, when asked by *Essence* magazine how his daughter enjoyed being an older sister, he answered point-blank: 'I only have a daughter.'

To add to his humiliation, Idris was filled with a deep sense of regret at having mentioned the child in public, knowing that he would be asked about him again in the future: 'To be given that and then have it taken away so harshly was like taking a full-on punch in the face: POW,' he said. 'You know, the truth is – like, even admitting it, I'll probably get laughed at for the rest of my life. But it is tragic, and it happened.

'But I wasn't knocked out. I stood right the fuck back up, and I ain't aiming to take another punch in the face ever again. Do you understand what I'm saying? It happened to me. I moved on.'

Shortly after this traumatic incident in 2010, Idris returned to London to shoot further episodes of *Luther*. In one scene, his character, DCI John Luther, is married but separated from his wife, played by actress Indira Varma. He hopes for a reconciliation, only to find out that she has moved on and is dating another man. According to the script, a furious Luther was called on to slam a door in rage.

But on set Idris was unable to contain the real-life anger he was feeling at the time: 'You have to understand, I had just gone through the worst thing in my life with, you know, the Florida thing,' he explained. 'So *Luther* came at a time where, you know, it was gaga therapy for me, man. Stupid. I was like, "I'm going in…" And that is what I fucking did.

'I tell you: I did that take, and I remember the room, Indira Varma, the beautiful Indian actress – beautiful girl. The crew were at this end of the room, all packed in. Indira was over there. And I fucking let go. Like, all kinds of shit happened in my head. I mean – blitz. Fucked up this door, I mean fucked this fucking door up. The emotion was going so long after the fucking actual scene was ended that everyone sat in silence. Indira was in fucking tears; I was in tears.

'The camera was still rolling. No one knew what to do. The silence just kept going. And then, finally, someone called, "Cut".'

And looking back on the whole sorry saga, Idris says he has come to be more accepting of the betrayal, which almost floored him years ago: 'I've not been an angel in my life either, do you know what I'm saying? So to a certain extent what goes around, comes around. But, for me in the future, I'm about being comfortable. That's it.'

He also believes that dealing with such a big shock made him look at his career differently: 'Now that I've achieved some of the things that I wanted to achieve, I'm not going to be a slave to it all of a sudden. I respect the artist that lives that way. The people that go, "You're going to hate me for what I just did, or you're not going to understand why I made that film or that record or whatever, but what you are watching is someone that's living their life." You know I'm not watching you, you're watching me.'

Fast forward to 2014 and Idris is excited about becoming a father again. His girlfriend Naiyana Garth, whom he began dating in March 2013, was due to give birth a year later and Idris was 'thrilled' by the news. On her website Naiyana describes herself as 'a London-based professional hair and make-up artist with extensive experience in Fashion, Film, special effects/prosthetics, Body Painting and Bridal', but it would seem she prefers to stay well away from the limelight as much as possible.

Despite Idris being understandably wary of settling down again, the couple try to lead as ordinary a life as possible. They had a rare public outing when Idris took her as his date to the Golden Globe Awards in January 2014, but he is the first to admit it can be tough to keep a relationship alive when he is away so much of the time: 'I've been in and out of relationships,' he said. 'I've been married, and it's hard to keep a relationship when you're an actor.

'A girl I knew said to me, "My dad told me, never date an actor or a DJ." It was over, right there on the spot; I was fucked. Nobody wanted to know anything about me when I was single but as soon as I had a girlfriend they wanted to know everything. I'm private and I want to keep it that way.'

He and Naiyana had made their first public appearance together a few months earlier at the *Harper's Bazaar* Women of the Year awards at Claridge's Hotel in London, where a source told *The Sun* newspaper: 'They've been together for a few months but it's really ramped up recently. They get on brilliantly and she's a real hit with his family and friends.

'Idris is known as a ladies' man but he's not really at all. He'd rather have banter at the bar than spend all night grafting on women. Although he doesn't have to try anyway, women flock to him.'

Indeed, Idris is finally so content in his personal life that he would even consider translating it onto the silver screen by starring in a romantic comedy: 'I'd love to do a rom-com,' he grinned. 'Get me in now! I could do my best Hugh Grant. I'm one of these actors who is not afraid of trying anything and I don't want to be pigeonholed. So rom-com, bring it, let's do it!'

But further heartache lay in store: just weeks after learning that Naiyana was pregnant, his happiness proved short-lived when he found out that his father was dying. Winston had lung cancer and, when he passed away in September 2013, at the age of 76, Idris was by his side, having returned to London from Los Angeles to be with him for the final few weeks of his life.

Of course, Idris was utterly bereft but his relentless schedule of promotion for *Mandela: Long Walk to Freedom* meant he was left with almost no time to grieve in private, and he struggled to avoid the subject of his father's death in interviews.

'It's weird,' he admitted shortly after the tragedy. 'My dad died eight, nine weeks ago. He was 76. He died of lung cancer. I am having to deal with grief and it has taken a profound effect on me.'

Despite his pain, however, he was determined not to appear ungrateful for his good fortune: 'I put on a smile, put on the suits and I go on the red carpet. I do the work, and I'm doing it because that is what my old man would want me to do. He was very proud of me,' he said.

Idris continued to work tirelessly and without complaining or asking for time off because he knew that his father, who had worked hard in a tough and thankless job throughout his life, would have wanted him to do the same: 'I suppose I am a workaholic,' Idris admitted after returning to work soon after his bereavement. 'This year's been weird. I've had massive emotional ups and downs. Massive. And the one thing that has kept me going is my work. It's knackering, but it's my outlet.'

Occasionally, his frustration with the rollercoaster he was on would show: 'I don't mind performing, it's just all the talking about it,' he sighed during yet another round of interviews in the weeks following his father's death.

Mandela: Long Walk to Freedom will always have special poignancy for Idris because it was the last performance of his that his father saw, just days before he passed away. Viewing the film together, knowing how very sick his father was, proved a deeply emotional experience for Idris and the rest of the family. 'He must have thought it was one of the last times he was going to see one of my really big performances,' Idris recalled. 'It's a sad film and now, when I think about it, it must have been emotional for him. He must have known.

'We were all in denial, it was a great moment to share. My dad was no crier so I kind of adopted that.'

Just days after burying his father, on 2 November 2013, Idris had to fly out to Johannesburg for the high-profile South African premiere of the biggest film of his life. But his schedule had been relentless and the emotional upheaval was to take its toll. Shortly after boarding the plane at Heathrow Airport, he suffered one of the most severe asthma attacks he had ever endured, and it terrified him.

'I sat on that plane and I suddenly couldn't breathe,' he recalled. 'I've always had asthma but when asthma hits you it feels like you've only got an inch of water. They took me off the plane because it was on the runway, took me to the ambulance and they took me to hospital.

'Asthma is one of those things that, if you've had it for a long time and you don't panic, you'll be OK but it was shocking for me. I've battled asthma most of my life and it just over-whelmingly took me down. It was a very scary moment for me. A doctor on the plane helped me through it. Thankfully, I am here.

'The next day, the hospital released me and the doctor told me, "You need to chill." But how could I not go to South Africa? How could I not turn up to the premiere? That would be nuts.

'This is the Rolls-Royce of movies, this is the Rolls-Royce of parts; it's the pinnacle for me. Yes, I'm tired but I'm saying I'll sleep when I'm dead because this is such an important moment, and for such a massive man I'll sacrifice.'

Since Idris never had the chance to actually meet Mandela in person, he later revealed that he had instead based his portrayal on his late father Winston: 'Not having met the man, my dad does remind me of what I imagine him to be in person: the presence, the humour, and the way he moves – elegant, but at the same time sturdy, a rock-solid guy. I channelled my dad's energies because he was a big fan of Mr Mandela and a union guy who struggled for the working man. Instead of a liberation struggle, his struggle was "My guys deserve steel-toed boots and a lunch break". But Mandela was always part of the discussion.'

And, in order to convincingly speak like the former South African President, Idris taught himself to mimic his father's speech patterns.

'There are certain ways that African men speak English, and Mandela and my dad sort of fall into a similar category,' he explained. 'They are very grammar-conscious and like to use long words.'

Both Winston and Idris agreed that, when he was made up to play the President in old age, he looked strikingly similar to his own father.

'Ironically, I looked just like my old man,' said Idris. 'I designed my Mandela on my dad.'

He has dedicated his performance to Winston because, growing up on the council estates of East London, he recalled that his father would talk about Mandela a great deal: 'We had a huge fucking crush on Mandela in this country,' Idris said. 'And my dad talked about him quite a bit.

'Watching my old man was part of how I made the transition

from a young Mandela to an old Mandela. It was about my dad, I had to embrace it.'

Until the very end, Winston had always feared his son was never going to have a steady life, and that his luck with acting could run out at any time: 'My dad was a shop steward at Ford,' said Idris in the midst of his grief. 'He was a real union guy: always fighting for the workers, and to anyone like that Mandela was a hero. Any time the BBC World Service was on in our house we'd have to be quiet if it was talking about Mandela.'

Idris first learned about Mandela when he was at school, but his father taught him a good deal more. He recalled: 'I first heard about him in Newham, at Trinity School. My dad was very much into what was happening with Mandela, very much an advocate for the fight, and I think he did a petition for Mandela.

'I was led by my father from a young age: this is Mandela, this is who he is and this is what he's done. That was always the backdrop of our household, alongside other political leaders. But Mandela stuck out as the one for me because he had such a compelling story: he was a man who was in jail. Why was he in jail? Because he was an activist. I didn't understand, I was a kid.

'My parents were quite politically motivated – well, definitely for African politics. It is an absolute inheritance, being African. It means a lot to my family. I'm half Ghanaian and half Sierra Leonean and the news of me playing Mandela is huge out there.'

Idris has followed in his father's footsteps politically, too. Having inherited Winston's left-wing leanings, he announced his support for Oona King in her campaign to become the Labour Party candidate for Mayor of London in 2012. 'I'm just an entertainer, and this is just my opinion, but I love Oona King,' he said. 'I think she's very smart and very focused and she'd be a great Mayor. I'm a proud Londoner. I'm worried that London has seen huge escalations of violence and I think she can help to break down some of these issues.'

There is no disguising the fact that family and roots are deeply important to Idris. He has a tattoo covering the back of his right hand, which he calls 'the black star of Ghana' in tribute to his mother's Ghanaian heritage, and in the middle there is a lion's face, which is the symbol of Sierra Leone – his father's birthplace.

'I grew up very British and very African,' he explained. His close relationship with his parents has helped him keep his feet on the ground. When he tells his mother that he has been working with Will Smith, or that Steven Spielberg or Kenneth Branagh has just called him about a job, either she does not know who he is talking about, or is just concerned about whether or not her son is being paid properly! While he admits his parents were proud of his success, Idris realises that they never fully grasped the extent of his fame and were shocked at the attention their only son received: 'It's weird because my parents don't really understand my business,' he said. 'I get fan mail all day long, but, if a piece happens to go to their house, they're like, "Oh my God, you've got a fan! You have to write them back. You have to do it!"'

And, of course, his mother Eve still worries about her son: 'She called me the other day to check I was brushing my teeth,' he smiled.

And it is thanks to Winston and Eve that Idris has always stayed true to his roots. Despite being an A-list star, he still travels with the small entourage he has kept around him for over a decade – his barber Brett, his godson Riaz and his genial manager Oronde.

CHAPTER TWELVE

ME? NELSON?

Making on an iconic role such as Nelson Mandela in the film adaptation of the former South African President's memoirs *Long Walk to Freedom* was always destined to raise Idris Elba up into the superstar league. But the actor freely admits that at first he actually refused point-blank to take on the role and it took a good deal of persuasion to convince him that he was the man for the job.

'I just felt like I wasn't up for it,' he explained. 'I didn't have the attributes.'

When he first heard that the director Justin Chadwick wanted him to tackle the role, Idris thought he was being wound up by pranksters, and that he could not possibly be serious: 'It was definitely momentous,' he said. 'I thought it was a joke at first. I was blown away,' he laughs. 'Me? Nelson? No way, no way! You want a real man, not a man from Hackney!

'I was in Toronto shooting *Pac Rim* and the producers called and asked if I would at least talk to Justin Chadwick about playing Mandela. I was like, are you kidding me? Honestly, I wasn't sure if it was a joke. I asked my agent, who is South African, and he was like, "No, dude, I've done the homework on this; this is the real film and they want you."

'I thought, "You can't be serious! You chose me out of every-one you could have gone to?"'

At first, Idris was in shock that the film's casting team had even considered him: 'I said that I look nothing like Nelson Mandela,' he added. 'But Justin came to Toronto and sat with me for three days and we chatted, and I understood what he wanted to do and I said yes.'

Idris and Chadwick spent hours discussing the nuances of the role, the burden of responsibility that came with it, and whether Idris felt able to do it justice. Initially, he told Chadwick that he felt overwhelmed by the role, and the pressure to portray Mandela accurately and sensitively was simply too immense: 'Morgan Freeman, Denzel Washington – these are the people that have time and time again given massive performances of this nature, but I didn't feel like I was worthy of it. I actually didn't respond for about two or three weeks.'

Like his screen alter ego, Idris has come a long way. And for him, receiving this offer was the confirmation that he had waited for that his journey from the council estates of East London to the very top of the Hollywood hierarchy was finally complete.

But, like Mandela himself, Idris has never taken any of his good fortune for granted, and was typically modest about receiving the offer: 'To call the prospect of playing Nelson Mandela intimidating would be to put it mildly,' he said. 'I couldn't understand why anyone would come to me. I didn't think I was accomplished enough as an actor.'

When he first heard via his agent Roger Charteris that the producers were seriously considering him, his immediate reaction was to turn them down flat.

'It was definitely no thanks. It didn't feel like the right time,' he recalled. 'I've got a career to defend and I want to be around for a long time. If I fucked Mandela up, that would be the end of me.'

'It's such a big character, a worldwide citizen, so it's definitely nerve-wracking. At this point in my career, do I want to take on a role like that if it then doesn't work out? That's what you'll be remembered for.

'I had doubts about playing someone so iconic. I honestly thought I wasn't qualified enough. I've had a good career and lots of work, but nothing like this. I thought, why Idris Elba? He has never been up for an Oscar, he has never done anything of this magnitude in film – oh, apart from that film with Beyoncé [the 2009 flop *Obsessed*]. He was amazing in that!

'I really felt that might spin me off into some sort of odd, not qualified, who are you? And even afterwards, it was difficult to decide what to do next. I love acting, I love performing great challenging roles, but they don't write many of those.'

Idris had many reservations, not least he was concerned that the lack of physical similarities between himself and Mandela would put movie-goers off: 'For someone who doesn't look like Mandela, you have got to work harder to get the audience in there,' he explained.

And he was understandably nervous about playing someone he described as 'One of the human race's most prominent figures of our time': 'It's hard to describe, you know? Growing up, he was this amazing, inspirational figure. His influence can't be measured. I can't put it into words,' Idris added.

But if he accepted the role it would be the first time a Hollywood movie had been sold on his name alone, and the thought scared him. 'It did,' he admitted. 'When this was an idea and a script and a negotiation, I was terrified.'

Gradually, however, Idris was convinced to overcome his fears and reservations by the project's highly persuasive director, Justin Chadwick.

He said: 'Talking to Justin Chadwick, I realised that, one, it's a massive honour, and, two, it's an opportunity to do something different from the average biopic. This is almost an origin story, taking you right back to where he began.'

Despite all his past successes, Idris still felt deep down that he was not a big enough star to be on the producer's radar, but then he made a rather surprising discovery: 'I found out Nelson Mandela was into *The Wire*. It's amazing. He might have kicked back and watched *The Wire* box set.'

Not only was Mandela a secret fan of Stringer Bell, but his ex-wife Winnie also remembered Idris from his heart-warming role in *Daddy's Little Girls*, in which he played a divorced father struggling to gain custody of his daughters.

Idris explained: 'The director Jason Chadwick had the privilege of meeting Winnie Mandela and Nelson's two daughters, and he played a guessing game. He said, "Guess who's going to play your dad."

'They all looked at each other and said: "Is it Idris Elba?" I was like, "What? Winnie Mandela knows me?" I think Tyler Perry's film *Daddy's Little Girls* is one of her favourite films.'

And, while still reeling from the shock of discovering that Mandela even knew his name, something almost as startling happened – Idris received a message from Mandela's daughter Zindzi, who told him that both she and her famous father were absolutely thrilled that he had been offered the part.

'I was nearly in tears reading that email,' Idris said. And, of course, after that, he felt he had no choice but to say yes.

Once he had agreed to take the part, he immediately set about learning all he could. He spent months researching every aspect of Mandela's background: 'It was deeply important for me to understand where Mandela came from,' he explained. 'Because we know where he was going, and that's a famous story, but who was he? Where did he come from? What was his upbringing? And that's what we focus on in the film.'

Other actors who have tackled the immense challenge of portraying Mandela on screen in the past include Morgan Freeman, Danny Glover, David Harewood, Terrence Howard and Sidney Poitier. Idris knew he had mighty big shoes to step into.

Bringing the character of Mandela to life on the cinema screen would be a milestone in any actor's career, but to portray the inspirational leader as a vibrant young man, just as Mandela himself was battling with ill health at the end of his life, gave the challenge an extra poignancy. Idris was understandably nervous about potentially ruining the memories people around the world held so dear, and destroying his own career in the process.

'Part of the reason I didn't want to take on the role of Mandela is because of who he was,' he explained. 'A role like that is risky. *Mandela* is pivotal for me because, if, for some reason, I couldn't pull it off or the film didn't work as a piece of art, that's all I would be remembered for. I am 41 and I really want a career – a long one.'

But, once he had signed on the dotted line, preparations began in earnest. The already formidably built actor began daily training and boxing sessions to look more like the statesman, who was a keen amateur boxer in his youth.

'I'm prepping for *Mandela*,' said Idris at the time. 'I've been training quite a bit as well, so trying to fit that in, because Mandela used to box. So, I've been boxing. There's not much sleep right now. Not many friends around me. There's not really any time. I'm sort of doing, like, 28-hour days.

'When he was younger, he was incredibly fit. He used to run four miles every day at four in the morning. His lifestyle back then mirrors my lifestyle now – just very busy.'

But Idris grew to enjoy the sport so much that he went on to appear in several charity boxing matches and is keen to try a proper match if his schedule will allow it. 'I'm actually training for a charity fight in the New Year. *Mandela* has gotten me so obsessed with it I actually want to fight,' he said in 2012. 'I'm two minutes away from commissioning a documentary about my journey as a fighter. Now would not be the ideal time to start boxing. But I just find it so fascinating, the conditioning. And I'm dog-tired right now, but I'm fighting through that. Usually I give up, I just want to go to bed, and will. I'll say no to interviews.

'But at the moment I'm using this fact that I'm working as hard as I've ever worked in a gym. It parallels the hard work that I'm putting into my film work right now. It's sort of like the discipline it takes to play these different characters is similar to the discipline it takes to get up and do two hours of really hard labour in a gym.

'So, I want to make a documentary about my journey. It's going to be a year. I'm working with two trainers, a boxing trainer and a fitness trainer. I'm going to bring them to me wherever I'm filming, from *Mandela* in South Africa to *Thor 2* and *Luther* Season Three in London.

'I'm really excited about that fight. My parents are from Sierra Leone and I'm trying to build this children's charity because kids there tend to die very young. I want to use the boxing as a way to raise money for it. Plus, it's just a huge challenge for myself as a man hitting 40. I won't be drinking at all. I'll be training all the way to the charity fight.

'I'm not a violent man. I can be, but I have to get over the mental barrier of, like, "I don't really want to hit this guy." My draw into it is about the physical challenges to a man my age.

'Everyone thinks they can box: "Come on, left, right – whatever". But the measure of sort of fitness is what's really incredibly appealing to me.

'When they say a fighter is fighting fit, I mean, if an alien craft was to come down and go, "We want the fittest people in the world to come," it would be a bunch of soldiers and a bunch of boxers and fighters. I'm serious.

'Their endurance and level of fitness is out there. I want to take my body there, I really do. I don't think I've got much to lose. I think me and my one or two charity fights, I don't think are going to change me drastically. But even if it did, oh well. There are characters out there that have crooked noses – I think I'll get those characters.'

But before he flew out to South Africa to start filming, Idris had to make sure he was fully prepared mentally as well as physically for the daunting challenge that lay ahead: 'During the six months I was in Toronto on *Pac Rim*, I worked on the performance,' he said. 'That included a lot of reading, watching a lot of documentaries, and trying to understand South African cultures, understanding that struggle, because I had never really read up on it.'

He travelled to South Africa ahead of schedule and immersed himself in the local culture, trying to learn as much as possible about the history of the nation and its relationship with their former leader.

Idris said: 'I moved out to South Africa prior to filming for about two months and stayed there for six months. I had to learn the accent, the physicality, the idiosyncratic behaviour, and so on.

'The role was definitely the biggest challenge of my life,' he said. 'I look and sound nothing like him but hopefully I've pulled it off.'

He tried to copy Mandela's mannerisms and pattern of speech as closely as he could: 'I spent a lot of time watching and listening to footage of Nelson in various stages of his life, although there wasn't that much in terms of footage on his younger life, but I read quite a bit and understood what that journey was.

'I did extensive work as well with the voice because I don't look like Nelson Mandela, which is a challenge for the audience, but I spent time making sure that the voice was as close to his as possible to give that sweet spot for the audience.'

Luckily for Idris, he was already blessed with an appropriately powerful physical presence, much like the young Mandela, who also cut an imposing figure. Mandela was well over six feet tall and rather appealing to the ladies! He was equally successful as a boxer and had worked as a hotshot lawyer before becoming the leader of a violent armed struggle.

'He's 6'3", he was a boxer,' said Idris. 'He's a very tall man. He became slighter in frame as he grew older, but at my age he was actually bigger than me. It's interesting because people don't know that.'

Although fired up from all his forensic preparations and months of dedicated training, when Idris arrived in South Africa to start principal photography and found himself on the massive set for the first time, all his initial reservations came flooding back: 'The hardest thing was doing scenes in front of South Africans, who had either been there with Mr Mandela or have a real perspective on apartheid,' he explained. 'Not looking like Mandela, not being from South Africa, and then coming in that room and making them see and feel the essence of the great man presented a huge challenge.

'I didn't really get over that. Basically, Mr Mandela had to do the same thing. He would step into these big cinemas and just stop the film and talk about revolution, change, causing trouble. It just so happened that people wanted to hear someone change the game.

'With me, I would learn my lines, obviously, but, given these lines are Mr Mandela's words or some form of his words, I had to put any reservations aside and just do it. I stopped acting and became the character.

'When I got on to set and faced about 600 Sowetans in Soweto, playing Nelson Mandela without a mask, I was absolutely terrified. I didn't look like the man so I had to bring his presence.

'But I put my heart and soul into that performance so I'm not frightened anymore because I did what I had to do. I don't fear it, I don't fear the reaction – I just want people to get the story and celebrate this man's life.

'What stands out about Nelson is his humanity and the fact that he had been treated in that way for his beliefs and still walked out of there with forgiveness.'

CHAPTER THIRTEEN

BRINGING MANDELA TO LIFE

Sadly, Mandela's failing health meant that Idris never had the chance to sit down and talk to him about the film before he died: 'I didn't meet him,' Idris said. 'Though I didn't necessarily want to meet him either, because our focus in the film was on a very young Mandela.

'Everything I wanted to know about Mandela was in a box somewhere or in a documentary. I am sure he could have offered insights to me that would have been poignant to my performance, but I didn't want to force that.

'I was very fortunate to have a massive support network that included his family and Foundation. If I wanted it, I got help with any question I asked.'

Idris did, however, meet with two of Nelson's daughters, Zenani and Zindzi: 'I had to find out things about him that made him more human. As warm as everyone thinks he is, in real life he was quite stern with his children. They said, "He's a great man but he's also our dad!"'

After seeing the finished film, Zindzi said: 'Idris Elba brings my father's essence to life with an exceptional performance as Nelson Mandela.

'I loved the film, especially how it portrays my father's life and his global impact from the values of a small village boy through to an international leader.'

Idris also had the chance to spend some time with Mandela's second wife, Winnie: 'Winnie said, "He was a freedom fighter but he is a man too, flesh and blood and he has flaws,"' said Idris. 'She encouraged me to be courageous. She said it felt like the first portrayal of her family that she had seen that meant something.'

And the transformation was so convincing that even Mandela and his closest family members thought they were watching the man himself! Zindzi said of her father: 'He had seen clips of the film and he saw Idris and he thought it was him.'

She added: 'When my 11-year-old grandson saw the movie last week I asked him what he thought, and he said, "The dude who played Granddad, when he talks he kind of reminds me of him."'

After agreeing to take on the challenge of the role, Idris tried to speak to as many people as he could about the late leader, who was such an inspiration to millions. Although he had closely followed Mandela's career when he was a child, he was surprised at many of the stories he learned about the former South African President during his research. And he uncovered a connection much closer to home – not only did he bear a physical resemblance to his father, but Mandela had visited Winston Elba's homeland.

'I found out that he had spent time in Sierra Leone,' says Idris. 'I found out that his handwriting was really beautiful and that we are roughly the same height. It was deeply important for me to understand where Mandela came from.'

He also arranged to spend a night in Robben Island, the prison where Mandela spent 18 years, which is now a museum: 'I wanted the audience to know what it was like once Mandela and his colleagues were jailed and the crowds dissipated.

'You know, a lot of people sort of know that he was an activist, went to jail and came back and became President, but not many people know what happened in prison,' he continued. 'And it was one of the most, I think, for Mandela believe it or not, the most liberating part of his life was being in prison and sort of reinventing himself, educating himself, re-educating himself and sort of building his patience and forgiveness for then to come out and become one of the most recognisable and significant world leaders the human race has seen.'

The experience of being incarcerated made Idris more convinced than ever that he had to do justice to Mandela's heroism. It was a long night for the actor, who by then was well accustomed to the luxury of five-star hotels, since he was given no special treatment. To prepare him for the role, his conditions were the same as the original prisoners. 'It was a shit hole,' he said afterwards. 'I had a thin blanket for a mattress and that's all there was between me and the concrete floor. They gave me a bowl. I had no water, nothing to drink at all.'

Mandela's cramped cell was so small that when Idris lay down on his straw mat on the floor he could feel the wall with his feet, and his head touched the concrete on the other side.

'I wanted to understand what it was like to have your freedom taken away,' he added. 'I can't compare one night, obviously, but your sense of appreciation for things is heightened beyond belief. I wanted to do this because I believe in what his message was – that we can all live together.'

Another significant milestone for Elba was turning 40 while on set: 'I certainly felt I had arrived because here I was, playing the greatest man on earth on my 40th,' he said. 'A ripe old age. If it is half-time, then I'm going into the dressing room with some oranges! A half-time break.

'It's encouraged me to prioritise what's important to me, family, happiness, not so much wealth, but having a sense of owning something and not just leaving this earth with nothing.'

On reaching this landmark age, Idris felt at the peak of his powers, both personally and professionally, and able to give his all to the role of Mandela: 'I don't have to protect some image I have as an actor,' he said. 'I just bared my soul in that movie.'

Despite his bravado, for Idris, the pressure to portray Mandela accurately was immense and he was concerned whether he had done enough to convincingly pull it off. 'People are going to judge me for this role,' he said. 'I don't look like Mandela. Some say I don't deserve it. Whatever. For me, it's important I am who I am, as I present this piece to the world. I'm 40 and I've had a great career; I'm all right to be myself at this point.

'Look,' he said, 'if I never work again, I don't care. I did my bit, you know? This film, for me, how can I top it? I can tell you the truth about me. It's easy to be honest now. I've got my flaws, I've had my ups and downs: this is who I am.'

The first seed for the film was planted way back in 1974 when Mandela, then aged 56, began writing his autobiography in secret. At that time, the African lawyer and activist had spent ten years on Robben Island, the notoriously tough prison six miles from the coast of Cape Town, across a stretch of water infested with great white sharks.

By day, Mandela was reduced to back-breaking work as he and the other prisoners were forced to smash up rocks in a limestone quarry, but by night he wrote. Each page he produced was reviewed by Ahmed Kathrada and Walter Sisulu, fellow political prisoners who had also been sentenced to life imprisonment alongside Mandela at the historic Rivonia Trial, when 10 members of the African National Congress (ANC) were tried and convicted of sabotage and treason after blowing up power stations and government buildings as a protest against the apartheid system.

Another prisoner, Laloo Chiba, condensed Mandela's notes into microscopic shorthand, and Sathyandranath Ragunanan 'Mac' Maharaj, a member of the South African Communist Party and a close affiliate of the ANC, smuggled the manuscript out when he was released in 1976, having hidden the transcripts inside the bindings of his notebook.

But, before Maharaj was released, Mandela buried the original 500-page manuscript in the prison garden, deep inside three empty cocoa containers. A few weeks later, he awoke in his cell to the sound of picks and shovels as workmen were excavating the garden in order to build a new wall. The manuscript was uncovered and Mandela was punished with the loss of study privileges for a staggering four years.

Eventually, Maharaj managed to send the manuscript to a contact he had in London, the anti-apartheid activist Lionel 'Rusty' Bernstein, who kept it hidden in the offices of the Communist Party where he worked.

After six months of house arrest in South Africa, following his release, Maharaj managed to slip out of the country and went to London, where he worked on having the manuscript typed up. He then took it on to the anti-apartheid politician Oliver Tambo, who was at that time based in Lusaka, Zambia.

On 11 February 1990, after 27 years of imprisonment, Nelson Mandela was finally released and *Long Walk To Freedom*, his autobiography based on the manuscript that he had secretly managed to write behind bars, was finally published four years later.

The publication was a truly momentous event, which Mandela feared he would never witness, and Hollywood producers immediately started a fierce bidding contest for the film rights. But Mandela had already chosen the man he wanted to lead the project.

Anant Singh is a South African producer, filmmaker and anti-apartheid activist. During his successful career, he had caught Mandela's attention several times through the 80 films he produced, including most notably, *Cry, The Beloved Country* starring Sidney Poitier, in 1995.

'I was very involved in the liberation movement at high school and started writing to Mandela then to ask if I could tell his story,' recalled Singh. 'I first wrote to him while he was still in prison, in 1988, and said that I was interested in making a film about him. And he said, "Would anyone really want to see a film about my life?" He is a very modest man – and a remarkable man.'

The two were introduced soon after Mandela's release from prison: 'He acknowledged the anti-apartheid work I'd done and we developed a personal relationship from there.'

Mandela granted Singh the rights in 1997, but the project was plagued with problems from the start and the film proved incredibly difficult to bring to the big screen.

'We felt such a responsibility to the subject,' explained producer David M. Thompson, who had worked with Singh on the 1992 film *Sarafina!* starring Whoopi Goldberg and about the Soweto riots.

The script went through more than 50 drafts, first focusing on Mandela's later life, then his early years, then as a whole. After five different writers had worked on the script, and numerous directors – including the late Anthony Minghella – had been involved in lengthy negotiations, it was Justin Chadwick who was eventually chosen to direct *Mandela: Long Walk to Freedom*. His film would use the screenplay by William Nicholson, who also adapted the movie versions of *Gladiator* and *Les Misérables*.

Idris himself was impressed by the way the finished script captured the true spirit of Mandela: 'I think the script does what scripts do, which is to map out a filmic journey, a love story between Winnie and Nelson. We chose to pay attention to who they were as people, then use that to reflect on what was going on in South Africa. This isn't a political film.'

The final script, adapted from the original 656-page book, attempts to tell the full story of Mandela's life, from his circumcision at 16 to his election as President of South Africa at the age of 75. As well as covering his 27 years in prison, the film also examines his decision to advocate violence, against the wishes of the elders who controlled the ANC, making him one of the most wanted men in the country. The movie includes harrowing scenes of his imprisonment on Robben Island but also reveals how Mandela was quite the ladies' man in his youth.

'He was always flirting with the lady journalists and he didn't mind getting into a debate,' smiled Idris. 'He would be polite but, if your facts were wrong, he would tell you. These are the things that influenced me so I could understand who I was trying to play.'

Inevitably, the film has to tear through the intervening decades at speed, but Elba's bold performance has garnered much praise.

For many years, Denzel Washington was in the frame to play the lead, but his schedule would not allow it. 'He's a friend,' said Singh. 'But at a certain point he wanted us to wait and it was a timing issue. I had meetings with a lot of big Hollywood stars down the years and they'd say, "I want to do it, but I'm not sure I can." Every actor is intrigued and they think, "Great, I can win an Oscar," but it's hugely daunting.'

When Justin Chadwick came on board in 2011, once the script was finalised, he mentioned Idris's name for the first time. Singh liked the idea but needed to get the permission of the Mandela family before an offer could be made.

'As soon as we told Winnie and the daughters, Zindzi and Zenani, they all said "That's perfect,"' recalled Singh. 'They knew *The Wire*. Zindzi even knew he was a DJ.'

And so the offer reached Idris, out of a clear blue sky, complete with the blessing of the Nelson Mandela Foundation. He will never forget the day his long-time agent Roger Charteris called with the news.

'My agent Roger is a white South African,' said Idris. 'And he was in tears on the phone when he called me. Do you remember when they did the lottery commercials, and the clouds opened and this hand came out of the sky and pointed? That's how it felt.'

As well as casting Idris in the lead, Chadwick also chose British actress Naomie Harris to play Winnie Mandela. She and Idris connected immediately, and the close friendship they formed is evident in the on-screen chemistry between them: 'Idris has this amazing ability to look at you and make you feel like you're the most important person in the world,' she said.

That amazing ability also meant that he was able to connect with the extras forming the crowds on set, just as Mandela had done in his lifetime. Chadwick would regularly put Idris in front of crowds ranging from 400 up to 6,000 extras at a time, many of them native South Africans who knew and revered the real Mandela, and Idris would have them genuinely cheering by the end of the take.

He also forged a strong bond with his director during filming: 'Justin wants to capture the moment, to get on with it, to drop the audience right in it so he can spin them around 360 degrees and they are still in the film,' he explained.

In one scene, Idris had to march into a movie theatre in Soweto and call the crowd to arms. It was a real theatre, with a real crowd of 600 genuine Sowetans, many of whom had seen Mandela speak in person many times and had found themselves moved by his passion. Elba, whose imposing 6ft 3in height helped him secure the role of a lifetime, found he was able to command the attention of the crowds just as Mandela had done.

Chadwick had them all fired up in anticipation: 'We're going to shoot this scene now,' he told them. 'Mandela's coming soon, be ready.'

Meanwhile, Idris waited nervously outside the doors for the green light to go on. 'We did our final checks, and then me and my troops walked in,' he recalled. 'ANC – boom! I had the haircut. Pa-pow! Young Mandela at his prime! I was fucking nervous, because this was Soweto. That's like someone playing Jay-Z going into Brooklyn, and he's not even from Brooklyn!'

'But I'm telling you, man, people were crying. First take, I'm not even joking. First they were like, "It's Idris Elba". Then "It's Idris Elba playing Madiba". Then it's like "Shit – it's Madiba!"' Madiba is the name of Mandela's tribe, by which he was often known in South Africa.

'It was so layered,' Idris continued. 'I had to fucking prepare those speeches, man. These weren't just lines, this man did this shit!'

Many of the scenes were filmed on a similarly grand scale: 'Justin has this great sweeping vision of the film. It's a real epic,' added the producer David M. Thompson. The director was absolutely delighted with how well Idris coped with the large-scale scenes: 'He was standing in front of crowds of 3,000 people,' Chadwick recalled. 'There's no CGI and no escape, he has to perform, he has to be that character from the moment he walks into the crowd. And he was electric, absolutely electric. 'The people loved him. He had many big speeches, big scenes in Soweto, with many of the people who had lived through the events we were re-creating, and they just loved Idris.'

However, Chadwick was only too aware of the pressure that was resting on his shoulders too. Mandela's highly complex life story had tempted many a movie-maker before him. The TV movie *Mandela and de Klerk*, made in 1997, chronicled the negotiations leading up to Mandela's release from prison. *Goodbye Bafana* (released on DVD in the US as *The Color of Freedom*) in 2007 focused on Mandela's fascinating and complex relationship with his prison guard, while *Invictus* (2009) told the story of how, in his first term as President, Mandela enlisted the South African rugby team in a mission to unite his country, which had been torn apart by apartheid. Although the film, starring Morgan Freeman and Matt Damon, was a hit, it still did not reflect Mandela's struggle in depth.

Mandela: Long Walk to Freedom is a much broader study of the entire span of the former President's life. The film looks back on his rural boyhood herding cattle in the Eastern Cape, all the way to a white army saluting him as the first black President in the Union Buildings in Pretoria, 1994. Apart from the occasional flashback, the story proceeds through his turbulent life, chronologically covering his journey from a young law student determined to make a success of his life to a political activist determined to die for his cause. After ageing through the decades, at the end of the movie, Idris appears as the elderly statesman, in his trademark batik shirt walking alone in the beautiful landscape of his childhood.

Both real and specially created newsreel footage is used to mark key events such as the 70th Birthday Tribute concert held for Mandela in London in 1988, and period music helps enhance the atmosphere. The movie cost almost £30 million to make, and, with a cast of 12,000 extras, it is the biggest film ever produced in South Africa.

The shoot lasted 81 days, and many of the scenes involving large crowds proved incredibly complex to shoot. In one potentially tricky scene, Idris had to give a speech to young ANC supporters in a rundown township in Johannesburg, from the back of a truck. The extras, wearing 1940s costumes, were all locals.

'We told them, "This is your story," and they embraced that,' said Chadwick. 'But with some of the riot scenes they got caught up in it. In one scene, we filmed some burning cars and I think a couple of cars were on fire that weren't meant to be burned.

'When we were finished, there was black smoke everywhere. It's a very raw country and there are some very raw feelings there, particularly in the townships. That history we are re-creating is very present and for a lot of those people it brought it back.'

'Perfectionism can be exasperating but he knows what he wants,' said one of Chadwick's assistants at the time.

Chadwick added that they relied heavily on Mandela's own recollections to portray many of the scenes accurately: 'We took all these images from his life, which had been part of our research, and he knew exactly where he was at the time, who he was with, what had happened on a given day. His memory is incredibly sharp.'

Of course, the main problem the producers faced was what to leave out. During his incarceration, the leader was unable to raise his daughters or bury his son. The production crew agonised over whether to include the heart-wrenching moment when Mandela's son Thembi dies in a car crash in 1969 at the age of 25, and he was not allowed to attend the funeral.

For Idris that was the most difficult scene to film because it reminded him of his own emotions as a father to Isan, who by then was 11: 'That was one of the toughest scenes I've ever had to play,' he admitted. 'I was in South Africa millions of miles away from my own daughter and it just brought tears to my eyes knowing that, if anything happened to my kid I wasn't allowed to run back to my kid as soon as possible, that would be heartbreaking.'

'How do you take a 90-year life and make it a two-and-a-half-hour film?' asked Singh. 'Everybody believes they know something about Madiba and that's probably reasonably accurate, but what they know only scratches the surface.'

Singh was determined to reflect the full sweep of Mandela's epic journey: 'He was being groomed to become the leader of the Madiba clan,' he recalled. 'Nobody knows about his life with his first wife Evelyn Mase, and we have highlighted the fact that he had a very traumatic life in those early years.'

Idris was made to look younger than his real age to play Mandela at the height of his political activism in his late twenties and early thirties, but the film does not shy away from also showing the darker sides of his personality back then, including the womanising and his violent temper. In scenes that were traumatic to film, he is even shown assaulting Evelyn – with whom he had four children, as well as another two with his second wife Winnie.

'Although he's a saint to many people, he's not a purely saintly figure,' explained producer David M. Thompson. 'In his early days he's quite a wild guy, full of fury and anger and passion and sex.'

Idris told how that time in Mandela's life is often forgotten: 'Your first reference of him is with grey hair but, before that, he was a fucking young rock star – girls everywhere, boom boom boom!

'He was one of the first black educated lawyers. That's like Idris Elba walking into Harlem Apollo when I was Stringer Bell. Standing ovation, wouldn't have to say nothing. Mandela went through that every day.'

The hectic filming schedule also packed in re-creations of key events in Mandela's life, such as the Sharpeville Massacre of 1960 when a crowd of around 7,000 black protestors converged on a local police station, offering themselves up for arrest for not carrying their passbooks. Overwhelmed, the South African police opened fire, killing 69 peaceful protestors, most of whom were shot in the back as they fled the scene.

The film depicts how the horrific massacre triggered a national day of mourning and protest, in which Mandela burned his passbook outside his home in front of hundreds of press photographers. It also shows unflinchingly how Mandela and the ANC waged a guerrilla war, and locks into a pattern of rousing speeches alternated with montages of either violence or celebration.

William Nicholson's intelligent screenplay deals admirably with this tricky material, presenting anti-apartheid violence in the context of the constant, brutal violence the white supremacist regime was meting out to black South Africans. 'For 50 years, we have been talking peace and non-violence,' said the real Mandela in his speech at the Rivonia Trial of 1963, explaining his call to arms. 'As violence in this country was inevitable, it would be unrealistic and wrong for African leaders to continue preaching peace and nonviolence at a time when the government met our peaceful demands with force.'

Thankfully, the movie does not sentimentalise Mandela as the world's cuddly old grandfather. At the same time, it shows why he felt pushed to radicalism by the appalling regime he was up against. And in the film Winnie has become so radicalised she does not question her husband: 'Fight them,' she tells him. 'I hate them so much.'

'I am terribly brutalised inside,' the real Winnie admitted to the BBC in 1986. 'I know my soul is scarred. But what has happened is that it hasn't brutalised me to an extent of being consumed in hate.'

The film could be accused of over-simplifying this incredible woman, but it is already two and a half hours long and it is not really about her. She remains a heroine to some and a villain to others, and either way is interesting enough to provide great material for a biopic of her own.

The filmmakers also recreated the Soweto Uprising of 1976, when 70 children were shot for protesting against the use of Afrikaans as a language in schools. They also manage to pack in Mandela's founding of the African National Congress' guerrilla force, known simply as MK, and his becoming its commander-in-chief. Other key moments are glossed over, such as the trade union movement mobilising mass campaigns of resistance and economic boycotts that, along with international pressure, contributed to Mandela's eventual release from prison.

While the political and historical efforts of *Mandela: Long Walk to Freedom* are impressive, it does underplay one crucial element of Nelson Mandela's personality: his natural wit. A classic example came in 1997, when journalists asked how he felt on meeting the Spice Girls. 'I don't want to be emotional,' deadpanned the man who had endured 27 years of imprisonment, ended apartheid, won South Africa's first real democratic election and ultimately became the most revered statesman on earth, 'but this is one of the greatest moments of my life.'

Considering the project had taken over four decades to come to fruition, Idris was faced with a monumental challenge, but the producers were not prepared to cut down on pivotal moments in the plot. 'It is a very difficult story to give a dramatic shape to,' explained Thompson. 'Five years ago, we seemed to be going nowhere with the script. We were too much in awe.'

When Chadwick was chosen to direct the film in 2010, he took a much less reverential stance towards the original material, Mandela's memoirs, and made some major changes to the script. He also decided to show how the father of the nation sacrificed his own children and a normal family life for his beliefs. 'I was interested in his relationship with Winnie,' Chadwick said. 'There was this electricity when they were together. He'd found his match. And that gave me the way in.'

Mandela first spotted Winnie Madikizela at a bus stop in Soweto in 1957. She was 16 years his junior, and the first black female social worker at Baragwanath Hospital. 'From that moment I knew that I wanted to have her as my wife,' he wrote in *Long Walk to Freedom*. They married in 1958 and set up home in Orlando, Soweto. Their daughter Zenani (Zeni) was born in February 1959, and a second daughter, Zindziswa (Zindzi), in 1960. Mandela had just four years with Winnie before they were forced to spend 27 years apart. They were finally separated not by prison, but by her hardline politics, which drove a wedge between them after he was released and had returned home. 'It is a tragic love story,' said Chadwick.

Winnie became more militant, endorsing the gruesome practice of 'necklacing' – which meant burning people alive using tyres and petrol. In 1991, she was convicted of kidnapping and being an accessory to assault in connection with the death of 14-year-old Stompie Moeketsi, who was accused of being an informant.

'I never stopped loving her,' Mandela says in the film, shortly before he is released, gazing at a photo of her as his 1950s bride. 'But you see, I love her as she was.'

Idris had the opportunity to speak to Winnie before making the film: 'She said to me: "Just make this film. You've done your homework, make it real." And she also said: "I see him in you." She's known Mandela since he was 41. I'm 41. At that point it's more than an acting job.'

When Elba was cast in this iconic role, both critics and supporters of the film were shocked. He was neither particularly famous nor South African. Many expected the part to go to a more established Hollywood star, and Idris himself was sharply aware that the film would change his life forever.

He described Mandela as 'South Africa's liberator, saviour, its Washington and Lincoln rolled into one.'

Justin Chadwick admitted later that Idris had indeed been an unexpected choice, for which he pushed right from the start of his involvement in the project, arguing against Singh's suggestion that Denzel Washington tackle the role instead.

'I wanted him from the beginning,' he explained. 'They were thinking of going down a more traditional route. And I said Idris has got great instincts, he's a star. There is something about him that has great subtlety and depth.'

It was a monumental challenge, and, although Idris never doubted his own talent, he was nervous about convincingly re-creating Mandela's distinctive accent, which is easily identifiable by millions around the globe.

'I couldn't do it at the beginning,' he confessed. 'And you know why? Because I couldn't understand what he's doing to make him talk like that. And it turns out it's his traditional language, Xhosa.'

Idris had to learn to click his tongue in a specific way, and use certain speech patterns to mimic the older Mandela: 'When he spoke to people, he took pauses. Big pauses. Like that. To make sure they understood every word.'

As a boy, Mandela is played by Atandwa Kani, but the physical resemblance is helped by Idris being tall – he is 6ft 3in while Mandela was 6ft 2in – but facially they do not look alike. Of course, make-up experts had to use prosthetics to age Idris over a time span of more than 50 years. As a young rebel, he appears in sharp suits, and ages gradually to appear as the dignified older statesman, lined and grey in batik shirts.

'I relied on costume and we had to be really detailed about how he looked, the way he wore his hair.' the actor explained. 'It was a long time in the make-up chair. Up to four hours every morning, sitting in the chair from 6am before I'd go on set. It was tough, I'm normally five minutes in the make-up chair.'

Idris admitted he was amazed when he saw his older face reflected back at him in the mirror: 'I was shocked,' he said. 'We did a really interesting journey designing the prosthetics.'

For him, nailing the look of the character was almost more challenging than the leader's accent. 'It was more Idris actually ageing than Idris turning into Mandela,' he said. 'The whole journey was harder than the accent. The accent is a continuous progression for me, but mapping out who he was as a young man and who he became as an old man was definitely a harder thing to do. What came of it was the older we played Mandela, the more I started to look like him, the more the voice, the characteristics and the walk started to come into play.'

Portraying a man over the course of his entire adult life was no easy task for Idris: 'Playing him at different ages was also a challenge – he had a different voice, a different energy as a younger man, and by the time he came out of prison his voice had changed.

'Justin Chadwick, the director, and I really paid attention to what that looks like, feels like, the age, the incremental moments in his life.'

To ensure he did justice to an epic life, to make it authentically African and to guarantee the film surged with drama and conflict, Idris spent weeks poring over footage of Mandela taken before and after his time in prison: 'I would literally watch with the sound off,' he explained. 'I wanted to do a good job, not an impersonation of him. It was an interpretation so the audience go along knowing I don't look like him but it's a performance.

'I start when he's in his twenties, can you believe it, and end up in his seventies. It's a long, mapped-out journey of his life, but it was fun spending six months in South Africa.'

As part of his preparation, Idris spent time among the people who had actually known Mandela: 'I went into the villages of South Africa to observe before we shot the movie,' he explained. 'I saw people my age and younger who knew me from my work. They looked me in the eye and said, "Idris, do you understand the responsibility you have here, pal?"

'That speaks about the culture and how they hold this story close to their hearts.'

At that time, the pressure of finding the charm and magic of Mandela weighed heavily on him: 'I wasn't expecting to be accepted as Mandela,' he admitted. 'But I knew I only had one shot. There is no messing about with this character or this story. We wanted to portray Mandela as a human being, including parts that were less flattering. We've seen the saintly Mandela. We take the audience on a journey prior to that to understand who he was and how he became the man who all know.'

For Idris, the time spent living in South Africa was critical to his performance. 'I stayed there to understand,' he said. 'It was important for me to be an observer. I began to feed off it. Anywhere and everywhere you turned someone could talk about Mandela in some form. These are people who have been through the struggle. I began to soak it up.'

And a key part of that challenge was understanding how people reacted to Mandela during his lifetime: 'A lot of getting into the role was about the energy,' Idris explained. 'There were scenes where I was told, "I don't want you to rehearse this. Just walk into the room and go for it. You'll feel it." I plugged into the energy of Mandela and the way people respected him.'

And although he never met Mandela, who died shortly before the film's release, Idris will never forget the man or the experience of playing him in the rousing crowd scenes. He described the vibe as 'palpable': 'You would hear the roar of the crowd of extras, and it just made your heart race. The energy of South Africa is just beyond words.'

Idris said the film's message is ultimately that any man can have a moral victory over his oppressors: 'Nelson Mandela realised that his oppressors were more afraid of him than he was of them. That was a victory too.'

Many critics have praised the on-screen chemistry between Idris and his co-star, fellow Londoner Naomie Harris who was cast as his wife Winnie. Harris had previously worked with David Thompson, Anant Singh and Justin Chadwick on another film back in 2010, called *The First Grader*. Their fruitful collaboration on that project, about a Kenyan man who first went to school at the age of 84, meant the team all agreed they wanted her as the female lead.

The actress explained that Idris helped her to deal with the weight of the material once she had agreed to play the second of the late political icon's three wives. When asked how she felt about tackling the role, Naomie said: 'It meant inhabiting places I try never to go, like revenge, hatred and rage.

'I don't hate anyone, and I'm really not a vengeful person, but I found it really difficult to switch off. Even after I stopped filming, it took me a while to shake her.

'The first thing Idris said to me was, "Whoa, what have we done? It's terrifying, isn't it?" It really put me at ease. We held each other's hands through the whole process.'

And just as Idris based his portrayal of Mandela on his late father Winston, Naomie confessed that she too was similarly inspired by her single mother Liselle, a Jamaican-born screenwriter, who instilled her with strong values.

'Mum has always been fearless,' Naomie explained. 'We didn't grow up with much money at all, but she was always willing to make brave choices.

'She instilled in me the belief that anything is possible. It makes for a very intense relationship when you have no other parent and you're an only child.

'If it has been instilled in you from a young age that anything is possible, you will ultimately come back to those beliefs, even when life knocks you down.

'I hope, if I'm ever lucky enough to become a mother, I am able to pass that on to my children.'

Naomie was as surprised as Idris when she received the call asking her to consider playing Winnie. It came as a total shock, not least because at the time she was in Turkey, filming the James Bond movie *Skyfall* (2012).

'They said the Mandela movie's been green lit, you're going to be Winnie and we start filming two days after you finish Bond,' she recalled. 'I said, "Really?"'

For her, the biggest surprise of all was that *Mandela: Long Walk to Freedom* was actually going into production, after 16 years in development with various directors and actors attached at different points.

'When I came on board they were thinking of Denzel Washington for Nelson Mandela,' she said. 'When they asked: "Would you like to play Winnie?" I said: "Great!", because, firstly, I thought: "I'm never going to hear from these guys." And secondly, I just thought Winnie was Nelson's wife. I had no idea how controversial she is.'

Controversial is an understatement. Now in her seventies, Winnie Mandela is simultaneously an adored icon and a loathed figurehead. She started out as an optimistic and apolitical innocent who became a defiant and furious warmonger, crying for bloody revenge. 'While I was filming Bond I had to do all my Mandela research and I was terrified,' Naomie went on. 'I thought: "What? This woman is like seven different women in one."

'I had no idea how intense Winnie's journey was,' she said. 'She goes from this innocent, sweet 19-year-old to a warrior leading her army, and she's embittered and full of rage.

'Everyone had such different ideas about who Winnie was. One biography painted her as a demon, another as a saint and I thought, "How can you create a cohesive character from all that?"'

But then Idris arranged for Naomie to meet Winnie Mandela before starting work on the film, and the two women met for dinner. Naomie asked: 'What do you want people to take away from this film? How do you want people to see you?'

Her reply proved extremely liberating for the actress. Winnie said: 'I don't want you to think in those terms. I want you to be totally free to interpret my life as you see fit.'

'It was nerve-racking,' Naomie recalled. 'She is a formidable woman, so it was scary to sit down with her. But she was completely different to what I imagined her to be. She loves gardening and has found peace.'

Naomie expected to be given a 'laundry list' of suggestions from Winnie: 'I would if someone was playing me,' she said. 'But Winnie was really cool. She said: "I trust you. Come up with the character as you see fit."

'She's so hugely complex, this mixture of tremendous warmth and compassion as well as anger and rage. She's a warrior as well as a nurturer.'

Like Idris, Naomie found the months spent filming in South Africa extremely intense. 'There wasn't a place I could draw on from myself,' she explained. 'I just had to imagine the sense of injustice I would have felt if I'd lived during apartheid. Not being able to have the same education as my contemporaries, not being able to sit in the same place on a bus. I'm a person who's all about justice and I felt the rage building up.'

Naomie's hard work and research paid off when Winnie declared that she was delighted with the performance. After watching the final cut, Winnie announced: 'The film is amazing and Naomie Harris's performance is beautiful.'

Naomie added: 'She made a speech at the South African premiere and was hugely complimentary, which was a relief because, if Winnie didn't like something, she's not the sort to be polite. In person, she told me she was moved to tears, that it all felt too real and she wouldn't be watching it again.'

Since then, Harris, who made her name with roles in the *Pirates of the Caribbean* franchise and *28 Days Later*, has not shied away from controversy either. Just as Idris was, she has been drawn into the race debate. And Naomie, who attended Cambridge University before turning to acting, agrees there are not enough meaty roles for black women: 'Going to Cambridge is one of the things I'm most proud of,' she said. 'In this industry, it's difficult to be taken seriously as a woman and that really helps.

'Obviously, there are roles that as a black woman I just haven't been put up for, like in *Downton Abbey*, but really the film industry's progress in terms of race has been extraordinary.'

Anant Singh was delighted when Naomie agreed to take the

part: 'She grasped the intensity of Winnie in a very powerful way,' said the producer.

Indeed, some posters for the film only feature Naomie, as her role is so pivotal, and they feature the tagline: 'The leader you knew, the woman you didn't'.

The film has gone on to become South Africa's greatest ever box-office hit, but it was almost not made in South Africa at all because of the lack of studio facilities to shoot the interior scenes, until Singh himself opened a new film studio in Cape Town: 'South Africa has great locations, great technical and creative resources, but the studio was always the missing link,' said Singh. 'I'd been trying to get one opened for a long time and I'm glad that we were finally able to do it.'

Since Robben Island, where Idris had spent the night, is now a museum, the interior of the prison was reconstructed at the newly opened Cape Town Film Studios. And, as most of the crew were South Africans, many of the scenes proved highly emotional to make, since they were often reliving their own personal experiences. Johnny Breedt, the production designer, said: 'We lived through all of this, on both sides, black and white.'

And Riaad Moosa, who plays Mandela's friend Ahmed Kathrada, remembers growing up in South Africa under the apartheid regime: 'We'd have to go to beaches where there were rocks in the sea and you could die. The nice beaches were reserved for whites.'

Mandela wrote in his autobiography that when he walked out of prison in 1990 he had one mission: 'To liberate the oppressed and the oppressor both.' And after so many years in the making, the production team felt a huge weight of expectation on their shoulders to create the most faithful telling of Mandela's story that they could. And no one felt the pressure more keenly than Idris himself and director Justin Chadwick who was tasked with telling the biggest story in South Africa's history: 'I've used the fact that I'm an outsider to come and research and listen for a really long time,' he said. 'Travelling the country, talking to both sides of the family, the comrades, the jailers, interrogators.'

He also had the chance to meet Mandela, who was then 93 years of age, at his Johannesburg home: 'I spent an afternoon with him and I will never forget it. You could really feel what he must have been like, this amazingly charismatic person.'

Singh was determined to portray the story as accurately as possible: 'This film, as much as it's entertaining, represents one man's ability, together with his colleagues, to transform a whole country,' he said.

And Idris is rightly proud of the finished product. He says: 'I tell you something, man, as arrogant as this might sound, I actually don't care what the press think. Because as a memoir to Mr Mandela, this film is one of the greatest gifts I think we can give to the Mandela family.'

The next step was the film's release in late 2013, and again Idris was nervous of the public and critical reaction. But Jason Chadwick heaped him with praise, saying: 'He's so inventive and he's constantly working. He wants to be challenged; he wants to not do the same thing he's just done. I hope he is offered parts that he deserves because there is so much he can do.'

CHAPTER FOURTEEN

TAKING IT PUBLIC

There were many strange coincidences surrounding the filming of *Mandela: Long Walk to Freedom*, such as the great man himself finding a clip so convincing that he actually believed he was watching genuine footage of himself, and Idris being convinced that he was haunted by spirits during the night he spent in the prison on Robben Island.

But the most extraordinary coincidence of all was when the anti-apartheid icon passed away, at the age of 95, at home in South Africa at the same time as the Royal premiere of the film was taking place in London, in December 2013.

Even HM the Queen agreed it was a bizarre moment when his death was announced to the Duke and Duchess of Cambridge at the precise moment when the first official screening was taking place.

'It was extraordinary because William and Catherine were at a film last night, which was the film about his life,' said the Queen the following day when she visited the Houses of Parliament to see a plaque commemorating Mandela's 1996 visit. 'The news came at the end. They were clapping away like mad and somebody came on and said, can you just listen please, we have just heard he has died. It's amazing, isn't it? During the first night of his film.'

It was the film's producer Anant Singh who had the unfortunate task of getting up on the stage at around 10pm to break the sad news to the star-studded audience. There were screams and gasps of shock from the stunned crowd, while others simply burst into tears. Idris then took to the stage, alongside producer Harvey Weinstein, to lead a two-minute silence in the auditorium as a mark of respect and afterwards the ashen-faced audience were filmed as they walked down the stairs into the foyer.

Speaking as he left the Odeon cinema in Leicester Square, Prince William said: 'I just wanted to say it's extremely sad and tragic news. We were just reminded what an extraordinary and inspiring man Nelson Mandela was. My thoughts and prayers are with him and his family. It's very sad.'

Idris emerged from the cinema just moments after the royal party, looking equally shocked by the revelation: 'I am stunned at this very moment. In mourning with the rest of the world and Madiba's family,' he said. 'We have lost one of the greatest human beings to have walked this earth. I feel honoured to be associated to him. He is in a better place now.'

Morgan Freeman, who had portrayed the great man in *Invictus*, was equally saddened. He said: 'Today the world lost one of the true giants of the past century. What an honour it was to step into the shoes of Nelson Mandela and portray a man who defied odds, broke down barriers, and championed human rights before the eyes of the world. My thoughts and prayers are with his family.'

Later, Idris had a chance to look back on how the events of that sad night had unfolded: 'Literally halfway through the film Mandela had passed and there was sort of a slight buzz around the auditorium,' he recalled. 'Interestingly enough, I guess, the Duchess, Kate, sort of turned to me and looked at me as she had her phone and I wondered what was wrong with her because she looked quite emotional, but the film's very emotional.

'I'm not sure what was going on and then I saw some phones being passed around, and Prince William had his phone and he looked at the message and I could see his face had taken a bad hit and I was wondering what was going on.

'And my girlfriend looked at me and handed me the phone and I looked down and there it was, Mandela had passed and it was on a website. It was just the most surreal moment. I looked back at Prince William and Kate, and they were just in tears with me. It was just odd, very odd.

'There's a moment in the film when I play older Mandela and he says this one line and it is, "Just open the gate and let me be free." And I kid you not, that was the one line when we heard the news that was on the screen.

'I burst into tears immediately and was so emotional and then we made the decision to go onto the stage after the film while the credits were rolling to make an official announcement to the audience. It felt like the right thing to do, but, of course, as I stood up and stood out, the audience wanted to clap for me but we had to hush them down and explain to them what had happened. It only felt appropriate to say what had happened and, honestly, there was an audible gasp in the auditorium. Some people didn't know, they had their phones off. It was just surreal.

'It was really, really moving. It was like church. Everyone was emotionally charged. It was definitely the biggest moment of my career. I have never had a standing ovation before and a film of this magnitude, a character of this magnitude, all rolled into this really weird, interesting space in my life in the minute.

'It was very odd, after seeing the credits and I walk on stage. They were giving me a nice round of applause but it was just this moment where I had to say please sit down, and announcing the official speech from President [Jacob] Zuma of South Africa. It was just weird.

'Friday was my birthday, Saturday I premiered the biggest film of my life and Friday saw the fourth episode of the third season of *Luther* screen to really big audiences in America for the first time. There are all these planetary things going on all at the same time and it ended up with that moment yesterday when everyone stood up and it just was like, "Dude!" We all just looked at each other, we were clapping and everyone was looking at us. I have never seen that before. It was amazing.'

But even before the sad news had broken, Idris admits he was finding the evening highly emotional. 'Tears were falling from my eyes,' he said. 'It was humbling just to be part of it. They wanted a great actor, not a movie star, which I'm not.

'I never met him but I was told he was pleased. He was happy.'

It was especially touching for Idris that Mandela was able to see a preview of his haunting portrayal just weeks before his health declined. He had been aware that the film was being made and was shown several early scenes before he died, including one of Idris walking up a hill and giving a speech. The scene is so faithfully re-created that Mandela thought he was watching footage of himself.

'He's seen parts, clips,' said Idris. 'One of the scenes is a long shot of me walking up this hill and giving a speech. Anant showed him on an iPad. And he thought it was him walking up the hill.

'Yeah, he's hearing the speech and he's like, "Oh! Is that me? How did they get me walking up that hill?"'

'I think he has been very complimentary about parts of the film he saw, almost in disbelief, like it has been done well. When they told him it was me, he laughed. That's a massive compliment on its own, you know. Game over. Thank you,' Elba laughed. 'So, whether anyone else sees this film, I don't care. If I can convince the man himself, that's enough for me.'

Reflecting in the aftermath of Mandela's death, Idris said that, although he had hoped to meet his subject, in the end his health prevented it and he was relieved that it never happened: 'I'm glad I didn't,' he said. 'Because I wanted to understand him from a different perspective. We had a great script, I'd read and re-read his autobiography, watched documentaries, done the research, but at the end of the day I had to do my performance. And I didn't want to do an imitation.'

Idris was understandably nervous and emotional as he attended a second premiere in South Africa: 'It was quite daunting,' he recalled. 'Big heads of state came out; Mandela's wife, his daughter Zindzi, Winnie Mandela, many other comrades from the ANC.

'And they all had expectations of what the film should be. I was overly aware that I'm not South African. If they don't like this film, I'll never be able to walk into this country again! But at the end I really got the sense they had been moved.

'The Mandela family loved the film. After the film, people clapped but they were trying to take it in. It's a very emotional film, especially if it's your own history. But Winnie said, "You're my husband now!" And she said to her daughters, "Take a picture of me and your dad!"'

Director Jason Chadwick added: 'Mandela's daughters knew

Idris from *The Wire* and they thought that he had captured the spirit of their father, his dynamism and vitality.'

There was also a special screening at The White House, when the US President Barack Obama invited Idris and his co-stars to watch the movie with himself and First Lady Michelle. The event was also attended by South African Ambassador to the United States Ebrahim Rasool and former US Ambassador to South Africa Donald Gips. The screening was arranged by one of the film's executive producers, Harvey Weinstein, who said: 'Knowing what a strong relationship President Obama has with President Mandela, it's an honour for this film to be shown at The White House.'

Idris revealed what a fun evening they'd had in Washington: 'President Obama said, "Tell Idris I'd like to see the movie. Tell him to come over and we'll play the movie." I went to The White House – they've got a lovely little screening room. I've been to The White House before but I've never been in the screening room.

'Obama walked in and he made a little speech. He said, "I'd like to thank the filmmakers Justin Chadwick, Harvey Weinstein. I want to thank Naomie Harris, she's done a great job. And then this guy…" I'm sitting in the back with my popcorn, thinking, "Hold on." He says, "This guy Idris Elba when he came to The White House last time, the ladies, the ladies couldn't leave him alone. So, ladies, I urge you leave him alone, let him watch the movie." It was hilarious. I was like, "Barack, stop, man!"

'He has seen the film and he loved it. It was such a proud moment for us to take this movie to the President. He was very fond of Mandela, they had a great relationship, so I felt slightly connected to that.

'It was a very special moment for me, these are two very special individuals and I sort of fit in there somehow.'

Naomie Harris was also among the guests at the private screening: 'Michelle and Barack are so down-to-earth,' she said. 'You expect them to be great but you don't expect them to be so personable. At the buffet, Obama came up to me and said: "You need to eat more, come on, fill up your plate."'

Once the hype had started to die down, Idris had a chance to consider the legacy he hoped to leave through the film: 'I want people to see the film,' he stated simply. 'I want people to understand it and then ask me questions because, without seeing it, people have already got ideas about what it should feel and look like.

'I am not Morgan Freeman, I am not Terrence Howard, and I don't look like Mandela. I don't have that sort of complexion and we are not doing a look-alike story. This is a real story and this guy, Idris Elba, happens to be playing him.'

In the weeks and months leading up to the 2014 Oscars, industry experts confidently predicted that Idris would be nominated in the Best Actor category for his performance in *Mandela: Long Walk to Freedom*. He seemed an obvious choice, given such an iconic role. 'People keep asking how I feel about the Oscars and I'm like, how can I celebrate when I've not even been nominated yet?' he said. 'Not to sound disgruntled, but first they love you, then they hate you, then they love you again: that is my life as an actor.'

When the nominations were announced in Los Angeles on 16 January 2014, there was a shock in store when Idris's name was not among those who had made the shortlist. Nor was *Mandela: Long Walk to Freedom* nominated for Best Film. Justin Chadwick was also snubbed by the Academy in the Best Director category, and Naomie Harris did not receive a Best Supporting Actress nomination for her role as Winnie Mandela, as many had expected.

In fact, the film was only nominated in one category, for Best Original Song, with the U2 song 'Ordinary Love'. The perceived snub sent shockwaves around the world, and there was a huge outpouring of sympathy for Idris but he was typically philosophical about missing out.

'Not everybody is gonna like you,' he wrote on his Twitter page. 'That's OK as long as u like yourself and the more time u take disliking someone the less time u have to like u.'

There was an outcry in South Africa, with many local people taking to Twitter and other online forums to denounce the decision not to honour *Mandela*. But, in an attempt to try to distance themselves from the backlash, Nelson Mandela Foundation's Sello Hatang said: 'The fact that the movie got a nomination for Best Original Song is good enough. Besides it's not like we are entitled to these things.'

And so Idris's plans to attend the glittering ceremony were scrapped, but he did not seem to mind about missing out on his red-carpet moment: 'It could be Grammy night, Oscar night, whatever – I don't feel the pressure to be there,' he said.

He knows he needs to be networking with the right people in order to be nominated for awards, but Idris tends to struggle to conform to the Hollywood movie machine: 'There's a fast track if you can do the networking. For some personalities it works, but for mine it doesn't.' he said.

He is still finding it hard to adjust to life in California, almost two decades after leaving London. Not only does the smog in Los Angeles aggravate the asthma that has plagued him since childhood but he also misses home comforts: 'I crave a kebab now and then,' he laughed. 'And not only that, but also giving the kebab man shit at 2am. "Bruv, did I say garlic sauce? Sorry you're gonna have to take it off." You can't beat that Saturday-night banter.

'I miss pubs as well. Sticky carpets, velour cushions. There's something about an environment like that where you can talk. In New York, you'll go to a bar and think, "What am I going to do, just stare at the birds that are walking by?"'

Despite his bravado, he was well aware during the making of such an important film that Oscar nominations seemed inevitable but he also knows the importance of staying grounded: 'You can't believe your own bullshit,' he said. 'The key to that is surrounding yourself with people that don't gas you up.'

But despite the lack of awards, and his attempts to avoid the Hollywood machine, Idris seems unable to avoid people who want to heap praise upon him. The film's director Justin Chadwick described him as: 'Brave, instinctive, he's got great truth'.

And producer Anant Singh has spoken of Elba's strong resemblance to Mandela, both in spirit as well as in person: 'You go into a room with Idris and it's the same presence that I felt with Mandela, in different ways.'

The team were of course thrilled when *Long Walk to Freedom* was nominated at the 71st Annual Golden Globe Awards in January 2014. *Luther* was also up for an award on the same night, so Idris found himself torn and had to choose where his loyalties lay.

'The problem is there's two tables to sit on: there's a "*Mandela*" table and there's a "*Luther*" table,' he explained. 'So, since I already won at the "*Luther*" table, I was going to sit at the "*Mandela*" table. But if I don't win that, I'm gonna run back to the "*Luther*" table and just be like, "Hey, sorry about that, guys. I got this one."'

He also broke the Hollywood taboo and admitted that he had been working on an acceptance speech in case he did win. Most stars feign surprise if they win, but Idris felt he needed to say something 'important' if he was recognised for his portrayal of the late freedom fighter: 'I've got to think about a speech, because you play someone like Nelson Mandela, you have to say something really important if you win. So, I've got to think about that,' he insisted.

Making a rare appearance with his pregnant girlfriend by his side, Idris looked dapper in an electric-blue three-piece suit on the red carpet, while Naiyana wore a glamorous floor-length gown, specially made to accommodate her bump by British maternity occasion-wear designer Tiffany Rose. 'She looked amazing on the red carpet, as she does all the time,' grinned Idris. He has always found it fun having to get dressed up for black-tie events, and during the busy awards season he joked with his fans that he gets turned on by wearing a bow tie.

Before attending the 25th Annual Palm Springs International Film Festival, he wrote on Twitter: 'My Bow makes my dick hard every time I smile...is that normal?' He then posted a second photo of himself adjusting his bow tie with a smile on his face, and captioned it: 'Had fun...releasing the beast..:) (jokes)'

The postings resulted in a tremendous response from fans, so he responded: 'Wowsers! Crazy how many new followers you get when you mention the D*** If I owned a Bow tie company I'd be laughing. Dickie Bows by Driis.'

Idris was delighted to find himself among a host of British stars at the Golden Globes ceremony since the nominations for the awards were full of hope for home-grown talent, with TV favourites like *Downton Abbey*, directing talent Steve McQueen, for *12 Years A Slave*, and acting heavyweights including Helena Bonham Carter.

Blue Jasmine star Sally Hawkins enjoyed a well-deserved

nomination for Best Supporting Actress in Woody Allen's black comedy, but she lost out to Jennifer Lawrence in *American Hustle*. Helen Mirren was similarly denied an award for her role in the TV movie *Phil Spector*; instead it went to Elisabeth Moss on the night, for *Top of the Lake*. *Downtown Abbey* was also snubbed in favour of the critically acclaimed US drama *Breaking Bad*.

Dame Judi Dench, Emma Thompson and Kate Winslet were also vying for a Globe, but all failed to secure an accolade for their respective performances in *Philomena*, *Saving Mr. Banks* and *Labor Day*. Also among the British nominees were Idris's *Mandela* co-star Naomie Harris, who was nominated in the Best Supporting Actress category. They were expected to contribute to a stellar year for the British film industry, but in the end the Brits came away with little to show for the evening, with only one award despite eighteen nominations. The poor performance subsequently dashed hopes of a transatlantic boost in the fortunes of UK film and television.

Surprisingly, Jacqueline Bisset earned the only British Golden Globe in 2014 for Best Supporting Actress in a TV Series thanks to her part in Stephen Poliakoff's BBC2 drama *Dancing on the Edge*. But the veteran actress struggled through a rambling acceptance speech: 'I want to thank the people who have given me joy, and there have been many. And the people who have given me shit, I say it like my mother – what did she say? She used to say, "Go to hell, and don't come back".'

Idris himself was nominated for Best Actor in a Motion Picture, but on the night he lost out to Matthew McConaughey, who scooped the award after losing more than 40 pounds to play AIDS-stricken pharmaceutical drug dealer Ron Woodroof in *Dallas Buyers Club*. Although Idris had impressed many critics with his performance as Mandela, in the end the judges at the Hollywood Foreign Press felt it was not enough. But the star was philosophical. 'Tonight isn't about winning, it's about the recognition of a winner: Nelson Mandela. Never forget,' he mused via Twitter. He added later: 'It's a difficult one because we all deserve an award for our performances.'

The movie had been nominated for a remarkable four awards but did manage to win one for Best Original Song – Motion Picture; an award that went to U2 and Danger Mouse for 'Ordinary Love', beating Coldplay, who were nominated for their score in *The Hunger Games: Catching Fire*.

U2's lead singer Bono said working on the film completed a decades-long journey with Mandela, having played at an anti-apartheid concert some 35 years earlier: 'This man turned our life upside down, right-side up,' he said. 'A man who refused to hate not because he didn't have rage or anger or those things, but that he thought love would do a better job.'

Idris also lost out on an award for Best Actor in a Mini-Series Or TV Movie for his TV series *Luther*, and instead that award went to Michael Douglas for his portrayal of Liberace in *Behind The Candelabra*.

Fellow Brit Chiwetel Ejiofor was another actor defending the rights of black people in his movie *12 Years A Slave*, the true story of Solomon Northup who was sold into slavery. The award for Best Motion Picture – Drama was awarded to his film but the actor himself left the Golden Globes empty-handed. He and Idris had been up against some tough competition in the form of Hollywood veterans Tom Hanks, for *Captain Phillips*, and Robert Redford, for *All Is Lost*.

Ejiofor was also nominated for Best Actor in a Mini Series for the BBC2 drama *Dancing on the Edge*, but the glittering ceremony had added resonance for both himself and Idris, who had found themselves pitted against each other many times before – much to the frustration of both actors.

He tried to play down the unwanted rivalry by congratulating his old friend on his nominations: 'It's really terrific, it's really exciting,' he said. 'I'm thrilled for Idris as well. He's gone through a remarkable few days with everything that's happened so I'm really thrilled for him.

'We've been friends for a long time now – it's been 20 years – so it's really exciting to have two projects out there. We spoke the other day actually, how exciting it is to talk about these two very different guys, Mandela and Solomon, going through these two different set of circumstances but they found them very embracing and found an audience in both of them.'

Ejiofor added that he had been delighted by the positive reviews for his unflinching drama, which also stars Brad Pitt, Michael Fassbender and Benedict Cumberbatch: 'It has been amazing, the reception and how it's been received by people. It's been remarkable,' he said. 'This was something I thought was just extraordinary and an amazing story. The opportunity to talk about Solomon Northup, his life and his experiences were so amazing to me.'

However, it has been tough for Chiwetel and Idris to play down the similarities that are often highlighted between them, since they have had much in common. Like Idris, Chiwetel grew up in London in the 1970s and 80s, where he too felt like an outsider being black, and faced racist abuse.

'I always loved London,' the actor recalls. 'Even then I knew it was one of the centres of the world. Oh, it often felt like everyone in the city was racist. We had to walk home through National Front marches. Institutional racism was just the norm.

'And it's interesting to think back, because, while my parents were coming here from Nigeria and trying to be useful to society, black people were subject to constant hassle – and now we see these reports about paedophiles in the public eye who were able to avoid attention at the time, while all the focus was on immigrants. So when I see "blame the immigrants" in the headlines, I think, "Well, who else is this letting off the hook?"'

His parents, Arinze and Obiajulu, arrived in the city in the 1960s as students fleeing the Biafran War. Like the Elba family, they settled at first in East London, before later heading south to Camberwell. His mother qualified as a pharmacist, and his father worked as a doctor, while indulging his love of music by performing as a singer. But when Chiwetel was 11, while on a family holiday in Nigeria, their taxi was involved in a crash. Chiwetel's father was killed, and he himself was left in hospital for 10 weeks, his forehead permanently scarred. For a long time he kept the tragedy hidden, but when he finally felt able to reveal the secret he admitted to a feeling of 'betrayal' that life was capable of such cruelty.

Like Idris, Chiwetel bases many of his characters on his late father, whom he says speaks through his roles on film. He based the everyday heroism of Okwe, the African doctor obliged to work illegally in a seedy London hotel in *Dirty Pretty Things* on Arinze.

And in the BBC drama *Dancing on the Edge*, his father's musical talents inspired his portrayal of jazz-age bandleader Louis Lester. Chiwetel was inspired by Arinze again for *12 Years A Slave*, the true story of a musician, father and free-born African-American in 1850s New York, who was kidnapped and trafficked to Louisiana, where he spent the next dozen years enslaved on cotton plantations.

And in another parallel to Idris's career, Chiwetel felt overwhelmed when offered such a meaty role; he felt a similarly huge sense of responsibility and almost turned it down, despite the fact that director Steve McQueen only ever wanted him for the part. But even McQueen's single-mindedness was not quite enough to persuade him: 'I was flattered, but that didn't conclude the journey for me,' he admitted. 'I felt intimidated by the part. There was a weight of responsibility, and a weight of self-doubt, and I arrived very much hoping Steve was correct. I didn't want to be the guy who fucked this up.'

He too has had to deal with constant speculation about winning an Oscar ever since the film first appeared on the festival circuit, but he has found suddenly being the focus of so much attention difficult to deal with.

'It's been very weird,' he says. 'Literally as soon as the film was screened, there was Oscar buzz, and that was very nice to hear. But part of me thought, "Well, hang on – this is a reflection on a man's life over 12 years of unbelievable anguish. Can we really dismiss that so quickly and start to speculate about awards?"'

Making the movie was a draining experience, as he likes to throw himself into his roles heart and soul, and, like Idris, always wants to feel what the character would have felt. He spent 35 days in Louisiana trying to create what he calls 'the Solomon and Chiwetel club' in which he could feel 'even a glimmer' of what his character went through.

More troubling still has been the press speculation pitting two black actors against each other. Because the media always want a storyline to every awards season – whether a foreign-language underdog or the veteran performer finally taking to the podium – in 2014, the focus fell on the likely competition between Ejiofor and Elba.

The contest may have proved a fascinating story but neither was particularly thrilled about it: 'I don't know what to think about that,' said Chiwetel. 'I mean, I am struck by how walking down the street I'm rarely made aware of my race, but that, among journalists, race is absolutely massive. I've read a lot of articles about myself that are just "black black black black black…"'

He repeats the word until it becomes a nonsense, adding: 'It seems a strange disconnect with the real world, and unfortunately it also generates a kind of racial tension.

'Simply pointing out that two people who have been nominated for an award happen to have the same amount of melanin in their skin doesn't seem very useful.'

Reading out an imaginary newspaper article, he went on: '"As you may notice, Chiwetel Ejiofor is still a black British actor…"'

He is understandably frustrated by the focus on his race. While race has been central to some of his big screen roles, such as his appearance in Steven Spielberg's *Amistad*, another film about American slavery, others have had nothing to do with it at all. He played a terrorist in *Children of Men*, and big-hearted drag queen Lola in *Kinky Boots*.

Like Idris, and many other black actors, he has made the journey across the Atlantic to find bigger and better roles although he still regards South London as home. And it was there that he first discovered his passion for acting. As a student at Dulwich College, a public school with a long theatrical tradition, his talent was spotted and – again similar to Idris – he graduated from school plays to the National Youth Theatre. There, a performance of *Othello* led to an invitation to audition for *Amistad*, and it was at that audition that he first met Idris Elba.

Chiwetel won the role, and with it came an 'absurd but wonderful opportunity' that took him to Hollywood at the age of 19. He now divides his time between Britain and LA with his Canadian actress girlfriend, Sari Mercer.

His relationship with the USA has been further bolstered by the country embracing his new film about slavery in the Deep South, despite it being made by two Londoners (director Steve McQueen is from Ealing).

And when he and Idris met up again on the red carpet at the Golden Globes, with his old pal about to become a father for the second time, Chiwetel was inevitably quizzed on the same subject. 'Well, I've always liked the idea of being a father,' he said. 'And I've always romanticised it, because I lost my father when I was young. In a way, all of the complications that come with my career are about that.'

Both Idris and Chiwetel have also been linked to a new drama that director Steve McQueen is working on for the BBC about the lives of black Britons.

'I don't think there has been a serious drama series in Britain with black people from all walks of life as the main protagonists,' he explained.

He was planning to develop the project, set in London, with a writer and a group of actors. 'This isn't a black *Our Friends in the North*,' he added, referring to the 1996 BBC drama following four friends from Newcastle.

Chiwetel was also nominated for the Best Actor accolade in the British equivalent of the Oscars, the BAFTAs, but Idris and his *Mandela* co-star Naomie Harris were sensationally left off the list of nominations. Idris, who was confused by Naomie's snub, joked that he would fly into a rage, like his character John Luther, at BAFTA headquarters.

Immediately leaping to Naomie's defence, he wrote on his Twitter page: 'Ok peeps, ...I've got an appointment at the @BAFTA I'm gonna do a #Lutherrage and ask where @NaomieHarris nomination?'

After it emerged that Idris had been left off the shortlist in the

Best Actor category, his fans reacted in fury. The snub sparked outrage on Twitter.

One fan wrote: 'No BAFTA nomination for @idriselba! What an absolute joke, get your act together BAFTA people!!'

Another posted: 'How is Idris Elba not up for a BAFTA for *Mandela: Long Walk To Freedom*?! Who the hell decides these things, totally outrageous!'

While another tweeted: 'Did the @BAFTA jury's consideration copies of #mandelalwtf go missing in the post? @idriselba may not have won but been robbed of nomination.'

Meanwhile, Idris himself masked his own disappointment to tweet best wishes to his friends who were nominated. He wrote: 'Congrats to @Oprah and Chiwetel @LupitaNyongo M.fassbender on their @BAFTA nominations. GREAT PERFORMANCES Well deserved.'

Despite the snub, *Long Walk to Freedom* was still nominated for Outstanding British Film, alongside the eventual winner *Gravity*, *Philomena*, *Rush*, *Saving Mr. Banks* and *The Selfish Giant*.

Idris downplayed the importance of winning awards, insisting it was simply an honour to screen the film for Mandela's family. He said: 'For us, showing this film to Winnie Mandela, and Zindzi Mandela, and to the people of South Africa, that was recognition. That's like as big as your Oscar can get, because they loved the film, they were very touched by it and so were we to present it to them.'

The snub by BAFTA was particularly surprising since, just three months before the nominations were announced, Idris had been honoured with a BAFTA Britannia Humanitarian Award at a glitzy awards show hosted by comedian Rob Brydon in Los Angeles.

The award, which has been previously presented to Richard Curtis, Don Cheadle and Colin Firth, recognises Brits who have used their status in the industry to highlight humanitarian causes and Idris was rewarded for his work as a knife-crime ambassador to The Prince's Trust.

Idris was introduced at the event by Mandela's daughter Zindzi, who said, 'My family and I were very happy when Idris was cast to play my father, as he is one of the finest actors today. Idris not only portrays my father brilliantly but shares his generous human spirit.'

Idris was presented with his award by actor Sean Penn, America's ambassador-at-large to Haiti, who got laughs by opening with the line, 'Idris represents a unique dichotomy: he's manly *and* British,' before turning to serious matters and noting how awestruck he was by Elba's performance in *Mandela*: 'I'm having a difficult time sitting next to Idris Elba tonight and thinking of him as a normal person,' he said.

When Idris finally took the stage to accept the award, he quipped, 'Zindzi, thank you so much for coming here tonight – and you can stop calling me Dad now!' He added: 'I wouldn't be standing here if it wasn't for The Prince's Trust. Honestly, I feel a bit guilty standing up here because I know I could be doing a lot more.'

'Idris Elba has used his success in Film and Television to turn the spotlight towards a very deserving cause,' said Gary Dartnall, the chairman of BAFTA Los Angeles. 'His work with The Prince's Trust for disadvantaged youth is highly commendable, and in complete accord with BAFTA Los Angeles' own work in the inner city.'

The Prince's Trust, which was founded in 1976 by HRH Prince Charles to help disadvantaged youth, had changed Idris's life as a teenager. As the recipient of a grant from the charity, he had been able to attend the National Youth Music Theatre.

Accepting the award, he told the star-studded audience: 'When I was 18, I auditioned for the National Youth Music Theatre, for the part of Big Julie in *Guys and Dolls*.

'I got the part but then they told me I had to pay £1,500 to board me around the world – they were taking it all over, to Japan and Scotland.

'I went home and told my parents I got the part but I needed £1,500. My father said: "Boy, it looks like you're not going, but good job. You did well."

'I thought, "That's not fair." But I had a wonderful drama teacher who I'll never forget, called Sue McPhee, who said: "You should audition for The Prince's Trust."

'So I did and they gave me £1,500 and they haven't stopped calling since!' he joked. 'The truth is they absolutely steered the course of my career and I wouldn't be here now if it wasn't for The Prince's Trust and that is why I spend time with them, and honestly, I feel a bit guilty taking this award because I know I could do more. A lot, lot, more. But you know these kids see me as a beacon.

'I go and I look at whatever The Prince's Trust want me to, but I know I could do more because young people need a beacon, they need to know their dreams can come true some-how, some way.

'I feel very proud to accept this award for doing that.' Looking at his award statuette, Idris added, 'I'm going to take it back to East London and show them we can do it.'

Since he started working with the charity, Idris has helped launch The Prince's Trust Undiscovered campaign, aiming to help young people caught in the recession.

The Prince himself was not present at the ceremony, and did

not send a message to Idris, but the mood shifted from serious to hilarious when Judd Apatow took to the stage to introduce Chaplin Award recipient Sacha Baron Cohen.

'No man has ever deserved an award more than Sacha deserves this,' the comedy producer said, 'even though this year Sacha did not create any comedy work whatsoever.' Apatow added, somewhat more seriously, 'He is clearly the best, the funniest, the smartest, has the most balls, or, at least the largest balls, the most observant Jew I know, truly a ground breaker.

'I love him more than Sean Penn loves Idris Elba – and Sacha does *no* charity work!'

After a series of clips of Cohen's work, Hollywood's Salma Hayek introduced a wheelchair-bound veteran actress called Grace Collington, Chaplin's oldest living co-star.

Cohen accepted the gift of a cane from the frail Collington, with which he broke into a Chaplin-esque dance, only to trip and send her wheelchair flying off the stage.

Idris was among the stunned audience who all gasped in shock, and then, eventually realising it was all a stunt, burst into laughter that lasted for several minutes, even as Cohen paid her fake tribute: 'Grace Collington is the oldest – sorry, *was* the oldest – I dedicate this award to her. This is obviously a tragedy, but, on the bright side, what a great way to go: giving an award to me!'

CHAPTER FIFTEEN

DJ BIG DRIIS

There is a photograph, almost four decades old, which traces back to the first moment Idris Elba can recall falling in love with music. Describing the old family snapshot, he said: 'I'm in dungarees, white T-shirt, four years old with a little Afro. I'm wearing African beads around my neck and I'm holding Marvin Gaye's *Let's Get It On* album, walking towards the turntables with my dad.

'Wicked shot. When I look back on it I remember being fascinated by the whole process of music.'

His West African parents, Winston and Eve, infused Idris with an early love of music, playing their only son everything from reggae, soul and the synthesised sounds of the 1980s to music with a deeper cultural heritage.

'They just loved to listen to music from their home,' he recalled. 'Not necessarily from Sierra Leone or Ghana but from the African diaspora. So you had Congolese music from OK Jazz, Franco, Tabu Ley Rochereau – at the time that Congo sound was very much similar to salsa or rumba or cha-cha.

'It would transform my mum and dad's home, this little apartment in Hackney, into this cultural, you know, you're on the ninth floor looking out and you're hearing this African music and you could be anywhere.'

Despite all his success in the glitzy world of acting, Idris is a man of many contradictions who has never given up on his love of music and still takes time out to perform as a DJ whenever his relentless schedule of filming and promotion allows him to.

Although he is probably still best known for playing the ruthless gangster Stringer Bell in *The Wire*, he loves 1980s pop tunes and would actually love to make a musical! He recently had the chance to DJ at a swanky BAFTA party and amused the star-studded crowd by avoiding hardcore hip-hop sounds, instead playing Madonna's 'Into the Groove' and 'Holiday' back to back. It was a legacy of years spent manning the mixing decks, which started when he was 14, helping out his uncle at weddings. He was bitten by the bug and within a year had started his own DJ business with some friends.

'I used to DJ for my uncle when he'd had too much to drink,' Idris recalled of those early days on the circuit. 'True story. I did it when I was 14! No one paid attention, so I'm doing it again.'

After moving on from weddings, his clubbing days began in local clubs such as Shanolas in Hackney Wick, its foundations now deep under the Olympic Park: 'I was spinning at blues dances and house parties around Dalston,' he said. 'Then I started going west, to Hanover Grand, then Club Colosseum and Twice As Nice. I love house music but I was brought up on Otis Redding, reggae, then hip-hop and R'n'B – I love it, man, it keeps me alive. I like to mix it up. I play specialist house music parties, but pop music always works. When you go to a club, you don't care who the DJ is, you just want to dance.

'The one record every DJ should have within arm's reach is

Michael Jackson's "Wanna Be Startin' Somethin'". You've got to have that, you can play it anywhere – you could play it at a funeral and someone will start dancing.

'I prefer DJing to doing press. I've always been DJing; it's just I'm making more of a push for it, making it more public.'

In 2006, Idris recorded his first EP, a four-song album called *Big Man* for Hevlar Recordings and he quickly began to gather a cool reputation as a DJ, even striking up a firm friendship with rapper Jay-Z, even before he worked alongside his singer wife Beyoncé in the film *Obsessed*. The pair found they had so much in common that in 2007 the US rap star asked Idris to produce a track on his album *American Gangster*. It was also the year that Idris was asked to DJ at the NBA All-Stars parties at The Venetian Hotel and Ice House lounge in Las Vegas.

He relished the chance to try his hand at a variety of skills: 'I have many different strings to my bow,' he declared. 'And I want to fuck around with them all. I don't just want to be an actor, I want to do other things.'

In 2009, Idris's music really took off. He was delighted to be asked to appear in the 'Respect My Conglomerate' music video for Busta Rhymes' album *Back on My B.S.* Later that summer, he was the DJ for BET's new series *Rising Icons*, and announced the release of his first single, 'Please Be True'.

He immediately started work on his second EP, which, he announced in *Essence* magazine that August, would be called *Kings Among Kings*, featuring six songs. At the end of 2009, he toured Europe and, just a few months later in February 2010, he released another EP, *High Class Problems Vol. 1*.

A keen singer, whose guilty karaoke secret is Bob Marley's 'One Love', Idris performed on the introduction to Pharoahe Monch's album *W.A.R. (We Are Renegades)* in 2011, and the following year he directed and performed in the Mumford &

Sons music video for 'Lover of the Light', in which he played a blind man going through his meticulous morning routine.

'I love being on set without being in front of the camera – it's a real creation sort of fest for me. I will be doing a bit more of that in the future,' he said afterwards. 'I remember when the guys called in and said, "Hey, we'd love Idris for a video that we are doing."

'I said, "Wow." Then they sent me an idea and I said, "Can I tell you guys, I don't really want to be in the video. I'd like to direct it. It would give me an opportunity as I haven't done much before."

'And they said yes, and there it was. It was an art-house piece of film, which myself and a co-director worked on. We fleshed out my idea of what it should look like. That is what came out and it was great.

'I loved the idea of directing. That interest has always been there. I remember when I was at drama school, you had to put scenes together. My teacher would say, "Right, here's your scenario, make a play about it." I got an A+ for drama.'

Idris also appeared in a one-off documentary for Channel 4 in August 2011 called *How Hip-Hop Changed the World*, in which he revealed the defining moments in street music and culture over the last 35 years, featuring rare archive material, seminal music videos and insight from hip-hop stars. In 2012, he fronted a Channel 4 documentary called *Idris Elba's How Clubbing Changed the World*, in which he interviewed the likes of Will.i.am, Paul Oakenfold and David Guetta.

And he enjoys DJing so much he has even considered taking a year-long sabbatical from films to focus purely on his music, although he appears to be too much in demand to afford himself such a luxury just yet.

'As an actor, you have to sell out where you're from because you're playing other people,' he said. 'That's why I DJ, because at least for one night, I'm me.

'It breaks the monotony of being yet another actor who can make it to a certain degree of fame. I'm rebelling against that. I want to be better, bigger, more, but I'm versatile, I'm an actor, and I'm going to keep making musical characters.

'It's not about saying: "I'm only making music" or "I'm only making films". There is a lot I want to do – I'm enjoying the music and we'll see where that goes.'

But Idris is the first to admit he prefers talking about music to his films; he lightens up, leans in closer and lowers his voice. To him, music is pleasure, and the films are work.

While working on *Prometheus*, in early 2012, he did not have time to take on any DJ gigs but he did have the chance to record some music between takes: 'It's my reset button I press when I've just finished a character and I'm preparing for another one,' he explained at the time. 'The thrill of playing music to a bunch of people and keeping them going – it gives me butterflies. I get butterflies when I act, but when you've got two turntables and 6,000 people in front of you, standing there going "come on then" – that feeling doesn't rely on the skills of an actor. It's all about instinct and knowing your music and reading the crowd. You don't get that from acting.

'I'm not out there to make money from it, but I get asked to do clubs and parties. I did Oliver Spencer's show at London Fashion Week, creating the mood of the show – it's a wicked extension to what I get to do. It's just taking a different form,' he added. 'I live virally more than I actually do in clubs now. I just DJ on mix-tapes and send the mixes out.

'I'm currently working on three mixes, house, dub-step and hip-hop, for *Prometheus* – and wait for it – I did a play on the words. You're going to look at the title and you'll say it says

Prometheus but it doesn't. It says "Pre-mixed for Us". Isn't that clever?

'Anyway, I'm doing a series of mix tapes for this film. I love it. I mean, in my bag upstairs, you'll get the clothes that I've been wearing for months. Then you'll get my little DJ unit that I mix in my bedrooms. Right now I'm using Traktor, which is a software made by Native Instruments. It's just a DJ software where all MP3s live on a hard drive, drag them into files.

'Funnily enough, I had to ask permission because I mean, I think because a DJ is kind of taste-maker and being in one of the biggest films of the year is a great synergy for both them and me.'

He spent the summer of 2012 playing a seven-week stint in a nightclub called Love & Liquor in Kilburn, North London, followed by a stint at the Flying Lotus club in LA and a residency in Ibiza.

It surprised many film industry insiders when he decided to treat himself to such a large chunk of time off, but Idris was adamant that he deserved the break: 'I've had an amazing year – an amazing seven years, really – and I want to celebrate,' he said. 'I want to DJ at home, in London. The truthful, honest way to celebrate is to get on the turntables and have a party.'

Whenever Idris is doing a set, gangs of groupies hang around the DJ booth to be close to him, and tend not to move all night. He admits that he would much rather they danced to his music instead of simply staring at him: 'It's a Catch-22,' he says. 'Until I'm known as a DJ, I'm going to get film fans pushing their way to the front. That's a work in progress, and I'm lucky to get that response. But of course I prefer a crowd who want to rock out.'

He delights the crowds who come to see him with nostalgic 1990s sets, which include Hardrive's 'Deep Inside', 24 Hour Experience's 'Together', 'The Cure And The Cause' from Fish Go

Deep, Wookie's 'Battle', garage classic Gabriel, plus more current tunes from Disclosure, Julio Bashmore and Ben Pearce. It's a strong, safe, high-energy set – and the crowd always loves it.

Playing alongside superstar DJs such as Fatboy Slim, Zane Lowe and Mark Ronson, Idris is in such demand he often performs three sets a night.

Taking a weekend away from his regular day job in August 2013, shortly before *Mandela: Long Walk to Freedom* was released to an eager public, he did an hour and a half at the Ushuaia Ibiza Beach Hotel, and as soon as he came off stage was whisked into a waiting car for a second set in the tourist town of Sant Antoni de Portmany. Once that was over, he was back to his hotel at 3am to start his final set of the evening, at Ibiza Rocks House at Pikes Hotel, despite not having slept in 24 hours, having flown straight in from Los Angeles.

The excited clubbers adored his house remixes of Lana Del Rey and Red Hot Chili Peppers, and, amid the slightly sun-burned dancers in shorts and bikini tops high on vodka and Red Bull, Idris was widely hailed as one of the most charismatic stars of his generation. 'I just finished a festival season in Ibiza,' he said afterwards. 'I play house and electro, which is quite a specific market. I love it. I use music in an interesting way. I definitely meditate to music beforehand, when I am trying to build an environment for my character to sit in; any kind of music. Then I use the creation of music as an exercise of my creativity. I am on the plane all the time making beats.'

When he is DJing, he is not acting or performing, but instead he likes to dive into the crowd, and have fun alongside them. Asked to introduce himself to the ravers in the nightclub, he yells: 'How you feeling? Make some noise! Fatboy Slim up later. And me… Luther!' When the crowd falls into a perplexed silence he shouts: 'I'm just joking! Grab a drink, have some fun.'

He thrills them by playing hits such as Madonna's 'Holiday', 'Kiss' by Prince and even 'Wonderwall' by Oasis, which is surprising since he famously had an altercation with the band's lead singer Liam Gallagher after the NME Awards 2011. The younger Gallagher brother grabbed Elba's wool bobble cap off his head in an apparently disrespectful manner. Idris took issue with his behaviour, and the two men got into an argument after he attempted to give Liam a hug and an affectionate rub on the head.

'Didn't like that,' Idris recalled. 'Don't touch his hair, apparently. Fuck off! Next time walk with a fucking hairdresser then. "Well, I'm a popular rock singer, so I'm going to be mean and fucking horrible to people just because they messed up my look." Fuck off! I played his song because his song's a classic. I couldn't, I don't, even know what his songs are about now or what band he's in now. No one gives a fuck, yeah?

'He was popular when he was in Oasis. He tried to have a go. Except it wasn't a fight, it was more of a banter thing. We had a laugh about it afterwards.'

Over the years, Idris has been discreetly recording music under the name Big Driis – quiet storm jams, rap bangers, deconstructed covers of Michael Jackson songs. For him, it has been a way of marking time and sharing certain feelings for which he had no other outlet.

Idris also sings, and many critics have found his deep resonating voice surprisingly tender. His debut EP full of soulful love songs was well received.

And his female fans adored the raunchier songs, such as 'Sex in Your Dreams', which begins: 'I'm in that zone, bone hard diamond-cutter/Dick thick, like homemade butter...' and proceeds from there.

'I'll be brutally honest in my music,' he has said. 'People will know more about me if they listen to my lyrics.'

To kill time between takes on film sets, he often works on tracks featuring the vocal talents of his leading ladies. He recorded a song with Violante Placido, who starred alongside him in *Ghost Rider: Spirit of Vengeance*, and Aimee-Ffion Edwards, a young Welsh actress who featured prominently in *Luther*. 'I have two songs that I co-wrote and recorded in respective hotel rooms with them,' he grinned. 'So my next project might be to get Charlize Theron [who co-starred in *Prometheus*] to sing a song with me. That could be my next EP.

'People see an actor making music and they're like, "What do you think you're doing? Stick to what you know." I think a few people were surprised when they enjoyed it,' said Idris. 'I just want to build it up slowly. I'm not in it to be a superstar DJ, I just want to do what I love. I've DJed since before I was an actor. Over the past few years I've collaborated with a few people and it's gone down pretty well.

'What I really want is to converge my film and music work. I wanna write the tracks for my films. And I wanna make a musical. I'm hanging about with the people that Baz Luhrmann goes to, I'm getting some great inspiration – it's something I'm taking very seriously. I already have some projects in mind.

'My music is really experimental. I put stuff out there and I have sold stuff and then I have worked on more specific albums with people like Jay-Z and Angie Stone, where the focus is to make a great track.

'I feel like music is always going to be a part of me and I think one day I am going to put out an album or two where audiences will be surprised. They'll be like, "It is not bad. It is a bit weird; I didn't expect him to be singing and rapping!"

'And the reason why I want to do it is I am DJing a lot now and my DJing takes me into studios quite a bit where I am listening to other artists. It is a bit like being a director. A DJ wants to be behind the boards and to make something because he knows how those beats add up.'

Idris knows there are people who lampoon his parallel music career. A headline in *XXL* magazine scoffed in 2012: 'Idris Elba still can't rap'. And others see him as just another actor cashing in on his fame to dabble in music on the side.

'I just ignore it,' he sighed. 'When I go off and DJ, it's my reset button. It's ppffooom! It's how I find myself. When I'm out spinning in a little club in Hoxton, that's nothing to do with film – it gets me back to who I am.

'I'm always going to be criticised but I don't care, I'm having fun. I know my crowd, I think I know what people want to hear and I'm trying to establish the idea that you don't have to be one person. If you have other talents, you should explore them.'

For many clubbers, he is much better known as a DJ than a film star and Idris loves creating alternative versions of himself, which is why as a DJ he uses the name Driis or King Driis. 'I don't care, you know?' he says when asked about his career that seems to suck up everything in sight. 'Ultimately, from my perspective, it all comes from the same source. Of course I'm going to be judged, I'm going to be scrutinised if I turn round and start rapping, or start DJing. But it all comes from the same source.

'The acting is more advanced, because that's what I've been concentrating on. But I don't over-think it because, if I did, I just wouldn't do it.'

Idris uses music as a way to unwind from the aspect of his work that he finds the most challenging – being interviewed by streams of journalists when he is promoting a film: 'I'm doing a DJ gig tonight,' he said after a recent interview. 'Why? Because I don't want to go to bed after speaking to 800 journalists, I want to play tunes and make people go "Yeeeeah!"'

Over Christmas 2013, he took a well-earned break from the whirlwind of promoting *Mandela: Long Walk to Freedom* and attending red-carpet awards ceremonies to make a special DJ appearance at London's Sway nightclub. He was invited to provide the soundtrack to a night of partying at the Covent Garden hotspot, using a different musical moniker – 7 Wallace. On the night, he was joined by American rapper Eve, whose singles include 'Rich Girl' and 'Tambourine', and former *EastEnders* actor Chucky Venn, who played Ray Dixon in the BBC1 soap.

He chose the name 7 Wallace because it was the street address where he lived while filming *Luther*. 'It was a party house,' he grinned. 'Even while I was working. I didn't have roommates but my house was big enough that all my mates moved in, practically. When you watch Season One of *Luther*, understand most of those scenes were with a hangover, which is what made it more grumpy and interesting to watch, I think.

'But 7 Wallace, everyone was like, "We're going to 7 Wallace tonight, 7 Wallace tonight". It just stuck as a DJ name. Was it planned? Yes and no. As soon as I saw the place, I was like, "OK, this is huge. I could fill it and have fun in it," and I certainly did.

'Well, it was basically I had all my mates, here we are in this big old house: "Let's have a drink". That's how it became. Then every other weekend, basically the turntables were out. We had a *Luther* wrap party at 7 Wallace, which was bananas.

'Interesting enough, when I talk about 7 Wallace, people always think it's about Stringer. Like, "Oh, where's Wallace, String? Where's Wallace?" Or they go, "Is that an ode to Biggie Smalls, Christopher Wallace?" No. But in 7 Wallace, we had a Christopher Wallace suite, which was the living room, which was for Christopher Wallace-type activities. You're going to have to use your imagination. If you know who he is, then you'll know.'

But his musical passion has a serious side, and Idris has revealed that his next album will be dedicated to former South African leader Nelson Mandela.

He said: 'The album will be called *Mi Mandela*. I went back to South Africa and worked with some great musicians. I'm really proud of the album. I'll wait until the film has died down so it doesn't get muddled but I'll release it in the New Year. Basically, it's a love letter from me to Mandela about me playing him. I took musicians from London down to Jo'burg and we are documenting the whole process of an actor making an album. I produced and co-wrote some of it about my sensations playing Mandela.

'The music of South Africa is amazing and I wanted to document that. I've put some stuff out before where I'm actually rapping but the thing is nobody wants to see me rap, I don't know why, maybe it's the English accent.

'I've always produced music, practically in my bedroom, it's also a discipline but I enjoy the process, it's a feeling, a great process, I love it.'

CHAPTER SIXTEEN

KING OF SPEED

Idris has also found another outlet for his creativity, relishing the chance to branch out into documentary making. A long-time car enthusiast, since way back when he illegally bought his first car at the age of 14, he could not resist the opportunity to meet many of his racing heroes when asked to make a film about speed for the BBC.

Late in 2013, he hosted *Idris Elba: King of Speed*, a two-part show about cars and car culture. In it, he explored how the compulsion for fast driving has influenced the automotive world and society in general, and examined the underground racing scene around the world.

He delved into some of the world's most popular motorsports and car cultures, meeting some of the top names in racing and seized on the opportunity to drive a huge range of vehicles from NASCAR to low-rider vehicles, via some of the most advanced racing cars and high-octane pursuits on the planet – all giving a unique insight into what makes petrol heads tick.

Having discovered his passion for speed at a young age, Idris clearly delighted in sharing his enthusiasm with racers and car fanatics across the world through his travels. He kicked off the first show by tracing his relationship with speed with a look back at his own humble beginnings, driving a Ford Fiesta XR2, black with a red stripe, around the streets of Hackney and revisiting the tyre shop close to the one where he got his first job as a tyre fitter as a teenager.

While filming at Uncle Tom's garage in Dames Road, he spent several hours with the current staff. Owner Tony Hunter said: 'He used to work at a garage up the road, when he was an apprentice when he was 16 or 17.

'We had the XR2 up on the ramp under a cover and then we took the cover off. He said it was his first car and then drove around the corner.

'It was amazing. He is such a nice fella and he hasn't forgotten his roots.'

That trip down memory lane was followed by an escapade across the ocean to Detroit and New Jersey, exploring the roots of speed and the impact of it on professional motorsports and popular culture. Idris spoke to ex-bootleggers, street racers and legitimate drag-race drivers, and got to thrash about in a 1934 Ford V8 – the hooch deliverer's choice of ride. Along the way, he was determined to actually share his vast wealth of knowledge on the subject with the viewers – like the fact that the origins of NASCAR, the wildly successful American racing formula, lay in whiskey bootlegging.

In the second episode, aired the following evening, Idris gave himself the goal of experiencing what he termed the pinnacle of motor sport: rallying.

He covered the history of rallying with Minis and the art of drifting – sliding a car round a corner at high speed without spinning out. Following this, he went on to interview folks from all parts of the racing spectrum, from Formula 1 to NASCAR to street rallies.

He wanted to drive a fiendishly difficult course in Finland and so he spent the first 45 minutes of the show gearing up for that task, by throwing a hideously overpowered Mini Metro around a track, learning to corner at speed in a Japanese supercar and getting the gist of throttle control on a motocross bike.

Making the *King of Speed* documentary gave him the opportunity to meet some drivers he had admired for many years, including rally driver Ari Vatanen, a Finnish former world rallying champion and bona fide legend of the sport, who invited Idris to spend the weekend at his home.

'I've had the pleasure of meeting some extraordinary motorcar drivers from a really wide spectrum of disciplines, but I think perhaps Ari Vatanen may be the ultimate,' said Idris. 'He is truly an extraordinary individual and, I tell you what, he is someone who will, right till the very end, continue to push the accelerator and break late on every corner, real or symbolic. He lives life to the full and you can see that when he gets behind the wheel.

'What stood out for me would have to have been staying with Ari and his family in the town where he grew up. We're talking rural Finland, which is very close to the Arctic Circle and is some of the most beautiful country I have ever seen.

'It's not anywhere I would have imagined I would ever have visited. I'm a city boy at heart, and to be able to take my passion for driving, do it somewhere so spectacular, such a world away from where I grew up and with someone I really connected with, was such a huge privilege.'

Vatanen, whose son Max is also a rally driver, proved to be a no-nonsense mentor. After Idris rolled his machine – with Max in the co-driver's seat – Ari gave him a pep talk: 'You didn't get to play Mandela overnight, so you won't be a rally driver after one day.'

Vatanen Snr's pithy nuggets of philosophy, added to lavish shots over the Finnish countryside and evocative piano music, made for great television. And it was a fitting climax when a clearly relieved Idris stepped out of the car to give his take on why Finland has produced more rally champions per head than any other country: 'They have no fear. They don't look at rally driving as risking your life, they look at it as maximising it.'

It was a sentiment echoed by Ari, who summed up his life, saying: 'I have tried to maximise each corner in my life, breaking very late – in real corners and symbolically. It means I make a lot of mistakes but I live a very intense and meaningful life.'

And Idris added: 'Cars, racing, speed, they are and have been for many people throughout history, a way of life; either a means to make a living, or a means to escape.

'I'm addicted to speed, it's no secret, but whilst travelling, listening, learning and telling these amazing stories, what surprised me the most was just how far people are willing to go, the risks people are willing to take, to satisfy that addiction.

'Rally driving is the ultimate, most extreme example of this; I mean you're not on a track, there is no wall of tyres to spin into, so, if you come off on that course, you're likely to hit a massive tree or roll down a ditch and chances are, you're going to get hurt. Bad.

'All of the drivers I met are willing to put their life on the line in the pursuit of speed. But it's not just about speed, it's about being faster than the next guy. As a speed addict, it's something I can relate to,' he said in a BBC interview promoting the programme.

Of course, Idris got behind the wheel himself as often as he could, and even tackled motorcycle racing: 'If people take one thing away from this documentary that surprises them or makes them look at kids on their streets tinkering around with their cars in a different light, then great,' he said.

'For some, like the drivers of the original Cannonball Run, cars were a means to make a political statement, to stage a political protest. For the bootleggers of the Prohibition era, speed was a means to make a living and evade the law.

'For me, my big realisation was that, behind the modern-day multinational car manufacturers and multi-million-dollar racing events, there is an incredible story. Because it's the risk takers, the moonshiners modifying their cars and the drag racers who were willing to bet shillings, muscle cars and pink slips, which inspired a fundamental change in manufacturing and led to the creation of some of the world's most popular motorsports events. That's quite a legacy.'

Idris admitted that travelling the globe as he researched the two hour-long films was quite an eye-opener for him, and he learned a great deal he did not already know about the culture of racing.

And, while something of a boy racer in his teens, he was intrigued to discover that kids are still up to the same tricks he used to pull with his pals: 'I think most people would think of "boy racer" as a modern term, but, since there have been cars, there have been boy racers,' he declared.

'Ultimately, boy racers are not just kids in their Fiestas down the Southend beach front, or the guy cruising around Chelsea in a million-pound Bugatti, they are all the people in between, who have been around since Henry Ford's time and who just love driving.

'I don't condone what they do, I can see why they do it. It is very exciting.'

And the actor could not believe his luck when the film crew

closed down an entire town in order to film at the famous NASCAR track, Watkins Glen in New York.

Since the track weaves through part of the town, the BBC needed special permission to shoot a sequence with Idris and legendary driver Rusty Wallace: 'It was quite extraordinary, really,' he recalled. 'Watkins Glen International has become home to road racing of nearly every class including F1, the Indy Car Series and of course, NASCAR. That permanent track was built just outside of Watkins Glen in 1956, but, prior to that, the cars used to race through the streets of the tiny village.

'We wanted to drive the original route so the production team got permission to close off the town. Racing is such a big deal in Watkins Glen, so the locals were really behind the idea. We had support from the local police and fire crews and everything.

'That car we're in, is a proper, bona fide NASCAR, so for the town to see one of those beasts burning round their streets was incredible. It is very loud and very fast. And Rusty Wallace is one of the greatest NASCAR car drivers of all time, so to do it with him was an immense privilege.

'It was amazing. I can tell you for certain, every speed freak has, at one time or another, driven through a town, looked at the streets and tight corners as if they were a racetrack and thought to his or herself, "I could have some serious fun if all these cars and people weren't in my way." And that's exactly what we got to do. It was incredible.

'But I tell you something, those cars are not built for the roads, they're not built to stop at traffic lights and they do not have a go-slow gear. In fact, there are only two gears. Go fast. Or stop. And Rusty went for it, he really threw that car round those blocks, I can tell you.'

Idris, whose passion for racing is clear throughout the two hour-long films, admitted that being driven by Rusty was one of the high points of his career: 'Let's face it, even with someone as experienced as Rusty behind the wheel, giving your destiny over to someone else is often more unnerving. Even with all that experience, you can't help but think, "This guy has had some of the worst crashes in NASCAR history and I'm putting my life in his hands". But then it's happening, and it's amazing and it's just... POW!

'Driving it myself was very, very different. You can feel right through your body how powerful those cars are. They're not called "muscle cars" for nothing. It took all my strength to keep that thing on the track.'

Although he had the opportunity to drive some of the most expensive cars in the world, Idris admitted that out of all the vehicles he drove for the purposes of the documentary, his favourite was the black Fiesta XR2, which he got to drive through the streets of London.

And, while he managed to fulfil many of his childhood racing dreams, he added: 'There is always another car to drive and more roads to race.'

But, of course, he remains loyal to his first love, the Mini: 'My first car was a Mini Clubman, I bought it when I was 14 years old – my parents didn't know I bought it. The Mini for me is a symbol of my liberation and being able to drive three different generations of rally-going Minis was an absolute dream – to be in those cars, a model which I've had such a connection with from day one, was a real honour.'

CHAPTER SEVENTEEN

THE FANS

Although he has legions of fans now, and is regularly named as one of the most beautiful people in Hollywood, Idris has not always enjoyed so much success with the opposite sex.

'To get that much love is a blessing, as an actor to have a female fan base is great but I don't understand it,' he said. 'When I wasn't on TV or in films, I didn't get any special attention when I went out. Some beautiful people always attract attention. I didn't get any until I got on television. So I'm on these lists only because I'm on TV.

'It happens to me all the time, still. I'll sit in a pub and nobody will recognise me. I might see an attractive woman, but she doesn't recognise me, so I'm not getting any love. Then one person goes, "Oh it's you," and suddenly they all overhear and start asking questions. It's bullshit.'

Idris was featured as one of the Ten Hottest Men on the Planet in the April 2004 issue of *Essence* magazine, and again in the November 2005 issue. He was selected as one of *People*'s annual 100 Most Beautiful People in the World in May 2007.

Then he appeared on the August 2009 and November 2011 covers of *Essence*, and on *Ebony* magazine in August 2010.

But even when he was voted in the top five of the Sexiest Men On The Planet by *Essence* magazine he just laughed it off: 'But is that me as I am, or because I am an actor?' he asked. 'I never used to have women shouting at me in the street that I was beautiful. I guess it's nice but I've still got the same old face.'

Despite the newfound attention, Idris claims he still doesn't get asked out on dates, much to the relief of his long-term girlfriend: 'I don't get hit on,' he says. 'I get a lot of female fans coming up and wanting to take pictures. But the actual "Let me take you for a drink", I don't get that.'

After enduring his fair share of heartbreak, Idris admits he has grown a lot less trusting of women over the years. When he was single, he would be approached for all the wrong reasons. 'The sex symbol thing, what does that mean? They don't want you, they want the fact you are famous; you are constantly having to navigate who's real. I always like it when I meet someone who doesn't know what I do.

'But then, the sad thing is, once they find out, you notice very quickly. It's all part and parcel of this game as an actor. It makes you less confident.

Before he settled down, Idris says he never found it very easy to meet women: 'When I was about 15 I could grow a beard, I was an athlete and I definitely got attention. In college, where it was all about being good-looking, all about performing, that's where I gained confidence. But I'm so shy now. I've been single for a long time. It's hard to meet women.

'Look, you probably think I'm shagging bitches all the time,' he laughed. 'But there's no way! They're all fans. I miss the days when me and my boys could go to a barbecue and go, "Who's that shorty over there?" Now *I'm* that shorty! If I see someone who's like – damn! – she's already on me and she wants an autograph.'

Idris admits it's becoming increasingly harder for him to live an anonymous life: 'I used to come to London, sit in the pub chilling and not get recognised. But that's changed,' he said. 'Today I went to the chippy, got a bag of chips and people are like, "It's that guy!" But people are more aggressive in America. In England they're like, "Ooh 'ello!"

The irony is I wake up every morning, look at myself in the mirror and think, "Whoa, I look like a piece of shit!" You watch yourself age and it's hard to feel like a sex symbol. Apparently, those days are for when you are a young man, and, yes, I get that thing, the litany of lust, I like that! But I'm not sure what it is they see, not to mention that, personally, I feel very awkward.

'There's no way all those women would ever sleep with me and go, "I really liked him." Some of them would go, "He was really boring or he was a bit aggressive" or, "Urgh, actor!" You know? But it's a compliment and it's a massive tool to use in sculpting a career, especially with what I do for a living, because I work in the face business. So it's a compliment and I use it accordingly.'

Like many actors of his generation, Idris has embraced modern social networking in all its forms. His Facebook page has been liked by more than 2.3 million fans and on Twitter he has almost a million followers; he also has his own website Driis.com, on which he blogs about his music and other interests. He used Facebook to pay tribute to Nelson Mandela when he died on 5 December 2013, posting a photo of the statesman with the message: 'I'm stunned, crushed, in mourning with you and his family, I feel only honoured to have portrayed him. He's in a better place now. RIP NM.'

And Idris was an early adopter of the Twitter trend,

continuing to update his page almost daily, sharing whatever happens to be on his mind at that moment. Often he delights his fans with philosophical musings such as:

'Here's a thought. If I'm not worried about YOUR shit but YOU'RE worried about MY shit, then YOUR shit isn't WORTH worrying about by anybody.'

Recently he wrote: 'Having a quality life depends on how much quality is in your life. Don't settle for less.'

'Be thankful that you're here today and enjoy those that are here with you. Truly. Properly.'

'You can tell when someone's bullshitting you by looking them straight in the eye. Never fails. ;)'

'Don't pick a lane, be a motorway, then choose a pace and use all lanes. Keep it moving. ;)'

Idris has admitted that he enjoys the recognition that comes with regularly updating his fans through his Facebook and Twitter pages, which are avidly followed. 'Things like Twitter map you,' he said. 'I don't want people to know where I am at all times. I don't want someone going, "I just saw him outside The Ship scratching his arse. Here's a picture to prove it!"'

Idris also uses the Web to keep an eye on his carefully crafted image, since he is a follower of fashion and always conscious of his style choices, which often include suits by Gucci and Dolce & Gabbana: 'I don't Google myself as much as I check pictures,' he admits. 'If I've been to an event, I'll check what I looked like. It sounds terrible.'

Idris has confessed that he is somewhat vain and works hard to keep in shape: 'Every man has that internal primal shit that makes him a winner,' he insists. 'The thing that makes him a loser is over-processing it. They say your first instinct is right almost all the time. But even if it's wrong the next instinct is to fix it, quickly.'

Being sharp physically as well as mentally is also high on the actor's agenda. 'I kick-boxed for six years but I never fought, as I had to protect the old boat race,' he says. 'But the fact I keep myself in shape isn't the reason I'm winning. I'm just thinking about doing the job I'm facing at that moment.

'I know the difference now between coasting it and applying it. I've always had ambition, and the acting was successful and put my name on the map, but it was never the plan to stop there.'

His ever-loyal army of fans are also leading a charge for Idris to tackle another iconic role – that of suave spy James Bond, but he is embarrassed by the idea, and hates talking about it. 'Bond?' he says. 'It is a bit like saying, "Do you want to play Superman?" Anyone would dream of it. It's one of the most coveted roles in film. I'd be honoured. But I don't know if it will actually happen. I'm just happy with the idea of being associated with it. It's nice there's a lot of goodwill.'

Despite his attempts at shrugging it off, the current *Bond* star Daniel Craig added fuel to the fire when he agreed that Idris would make the perfect successor as 007.

'Apparently, Daniel Craig said I'd be a great Bond. Daniel, why did you say that? Dropped me right in it! What an honour it would be, but also, what an indication of change,' said Idris. 'I know Ian Fleming lived in Jamaica for a long time, didn't he? I think it's interesting to think what he would have made of a black man playing Bond.

'If they thought I was self-campaigning, it would be such a turn-off,' said Idris, with typical modesty, determined to rebel against all the hype. 'I've been advised to pipe down.'

There is an article on the Internet entitled 'Five Questions You Should Never Ask Idris Elba'. And number one is 'Don't ask him about being the black James Bond'. It is the black part, not the Bond part, which bothers him so much.

'I've always detested the phrase "black Bond", I just don't understand it,' said Idris. 'We don't say "white Bond", we just say "Bond", so it suddenly becomes a black man and he's a "black Bond". So I hate that phrase and it's a rumour that has gotten out of control basically, but that's all it is. There's no truth in it whatsoever.

'Sean Connery wasn't the Scottish James Bond and Daniel Craig wasn't the blue-eyed James Bond. So, if I played him, I don't want to be called the black James Bond.'

Idris thinks the idea is so controversial only because audiences find it difficult to see a star step out of their comfort zone and try their hand at something they have never done before. 'My ambition has always been massive,' he reflected. 'I was known for hard work and I wanted to work on different things. I know people criticised that – stay in your lane, do what you're good at. But I'm not satisfied with that. I have ambitions to produce music and films, to direct, own a couple of restaurants. There's no rules to say I can't do that, but one can thwart one's own ambition by listening to people saying, "Stay in your lane, you're doing too much". I don't believe in that.'

But the rumours of his taking over the role ramped up another notch when his *Mandela* co-star Naomie Harris let slip that Idris was being considered by the Bond producers.

She said later: 'A journalist once asked me, "Who do you think is going to be the next Bond?" I said, "I've just finished working with Idris so, if I had the chance, I would vote for him."

'The next thing there were headlines going: "Naomie Harris says Idris Elba to be the next Bond". And Idris has had to live with that ever since. Now, nearly every time he does an interview, he gets asked about it.'

Naomie herself has been a pioneer in changing roles for black women, not least in transforming the traditional simpering

Bond Girl into a gun-toting Bond Woman, as she insists she's called. In 2014, shooting began on the franchise's 24th film, where she plays a 21st-century Miss Moneypenny: 'I don't know anything about the script, which is great, because I can't reveal anything,' she grinned.

And Idris had to eventually admit that he was intrigued by the idea of tackling Bond: 'The English are good at bad guys,' he said. 'The James Bond-style villain – cunning, slow-burning. The Americans are much more obvious about it.

'If it fucking happens, it's the will of the nation,' he added. 'It's not because of me. Everywhere I go people are saying, "You'd be a great Bond". And I want to ask them, "Are you saying that because it's trendy or because you mean it?" But you can tell by the look in their eyes. They mean it!

'I'm rebelling against being handed a career like "You're the next this; you're the next that". I'm not the next anything, I'm the first me. I can't be myself, I can't just be Idris Elba, but that's just the nature of the business.'

CHAPTER EIGHTEEN

THE FUTURE'S BRIGHT

Idris is now in the enviable position of owning several homes dotted around the globe, and divides his time between his mother in London, work commitments in Hollywood and his daughter Isan, who now lives in Atlanta, although he has confessed that they often end up meeting in hotel rooms in New York or Los Angeles. 'We've had this relationship since she was one,' he explains. 'She's always on the road.'

Although it sounds unconventional, Idris claims to be very much a traditional father to Isan, even though he cannot be with her as much as he would like: 'I'm very protective of my daughter and who she hangs out with,' he said. 'You can drive yourself nuts as a parent, thinking about what boys do and what I got up to as a kid. If my kid got up to that same stuff, I'd be horrified.'

He tries to get to Atlanta to see Isan whenever his schedule will allow him a few days to himself: 'I don't live there, I just own a home there and my daughter, Isan, lives with family there,' he explained. 'I'm in and out there, and she's in and out to see me. It takes a lot of organisation; sort of time management, basically. It doesn't feel as organic as normal parenting. It's like, "Oh, Dad, can I talk to you?" "Yeah." You have to sort of allocate time and do things in a way that allows me and her to hang out.

'But we manage it. The shoot for *No Good Deed* was definitely designed so that I could be at home for a while.

'I hug trees,' Idris added. 'I've got a tree tattooed on my arm. My daughter and I, every New Year's if we're together, we go out at the stroke of midnight and we go sit by a tree and have a picnic and chat.'

Now she is old enough to fully understand what he does for a living, Idris would like to make films that Isan can actually watch, since all the work he has done to date would be somewhat unsuitable viewing.

'I love kids and kids like me, so I'd like to do something a bit silly in that world,' he said. 'I admire Dwayne Johnson, the Rock, and his fearlessness in taking roles like that even though he's known for being a hard man.

'That shows versatility. He has a fearless approach to playing roles that are the opposite of that. That's great to me; I like him, I like that. Plus those movies are a lot of fun, and my daughter loves those type of films.

'I haven't done many comedies. I'd like to do some films skewed towards children. I'm not getting offered roles by Disney at all but I'd love to try something like that.'

It may also surprise fans of Stringer Bell and John Luther to learn that Idris would also relish the chance to try his hand at an all-singing, all-dancing show: 'In future, I want to do a musical,' he said. 'I want to do things that challenge me. I've got a keen eye on music and would like to do something that marries my world of acting and music. I am not sure if I can sing very well but I will be good – I promise! I will be captivating.

'I have done the stage in the past sporadically throughout my career. In the future, I'd like to do it. The problem with theatre is that I have a short attention span so I can't do it for six months or whatever.

'I've got the philosophy that I want to do everything at least once,' he says. 'I haven't had the opportunity to do a Kung Fu film yet, but, trust me, I will get one at some point. What's the point in being an actor if you play the same role over and over again?

'I'm not a clown who puts on a face and does the same routine every night, I'm supposed to try and depict every single person I can.'

Aside from acting, Idris also has plans for charity work to honour his late father Winston: 'I want to go to Sierra Leone with something,' he said, 'whether it's some sort of contribution to healthcare or to the entertainment industry. My cousin is a nurse, we are talking about opening a clinic.'

And he is delighted to find himself secure enough financially to be able to donate a hefty chunk to charity. He has enough money to retire but Idris has never really been bothered by the size of his bank balance: 'To me, money represents freedom,' he says. 'It represents being able to say no, to provide for my family.

'I'm still working class, still busting my arse working hard for money. I feel that my journey has been one of extreme hard work and I believe in dreaming.

'I believe in fulfilling your own destiny and it feels great to know that I'd wanted to have this sort of career and now here I am. It wasn't handed to me, I just knew I wanted to get it and didn't know how I was going to get it, but I saw my way through and it feels good.

'Twenty or thirty years from now, I'm going to be on a beach in Jamaica.'

But Idris still has an enormous amount that he wants to achieve before we find him swinging in a hammock between two palm trees: 'My ambition is what took me out to the States,' he says. 'I wanted to achieve something that hadn't been achieved. I wanted to avoid stereotypes. But that meant this was gonna be a slow-burn career. And hey, man, I wanna be around for a little while! I'd love to be able to make films until the day I die.'

With his mother recently widowed, Idris is planning to spend more time in London. He has also produced a British teen-slasher movie, called *Suicide Kids*, and BBC2 has commissioned him to direct a 90-minute film set in the streets of Hackney where he grew up, called *Second Coming*. 'It's a small tale about a young girl that I've been working on for about a year,' he explained. 'I'm not writing it, but I'm helping shape the script and hopefully we'll get to work on it at the end of this year.

'I've been acting for 20 years. What keeps me going is the fact that I want to do something I haven't done before. I'm not a household name and I love that because it keeps me, it allows me to keep growing and breathing. No one goes, "Oh, it's Idris Elba's movie". Or "It's an Elba picture", or "It's typical Elba".

'At this point, even though the films are getting bigger, I'm not getting more famous. That's an interesting position to be in as an actor. You're doing more, you're recognised as a great actor, but you're not a household name.'

And, although he wants to produce and direct, Idris is not sure he could lead a team. Speaking about himself in the third person, as he often does, he said: 'I think Idris Elba, in reality, I don't know if I'm a leader.

'I don't follow many people. I lead myself, if you like. I'm one of those people that, if I was to sit on a team and the team leader was no good, I'd quickly switch off. I would be like, "No. I'm going to do something else".

'I wouldn't become the leader, though.'

But Idris knows how fortunate he has been to work steadily through the years, since *The Wire* gave him his big break. Looking back, he smiles: 'My work sounds like a verse by some braggadocious rapper: "I kicked it with Beyoncé, then I kicked it with Charlize Theron and Ridley Scott and Denzel..."

'I've been living in LA, in Miami, in Brooklyn, in East London. It all gives me a unique perspective as an actor, as a director. It's rare to be in that position – and it's what makes me tick.'

He is now in a position to pick and choose the roles he likes, and he knows how to select the best opportunities that come his way: 'It's largely the character,' he explains. 'In hindsight, my characters have been varied, but the films perhaps haven't been up to the standard of the characters.

'So, going forward, I am still looking for challenging roles, but at the same time I want to keep an eye out for what the films mean and say.'

Idris says playing Mandela has changed him and made him reconsider the type of roles he is prepared to accept: 'I want to play another character that is compelling, and I am about to do a film with Cary Fukunaga about child soldiers in a West African civil war [based on Uzodinma's 2005 fictional novel *Beasts of No Nation*]. This character is nothing like Mandela, he is an awful, awful man. For me, that's a challenge.

'Stringer Bell was pretty awful, but he's a psychopathic soldier who told children they could be soldiers. It's awful. Well, that's what I want to do with him.'

The drama, also called *Beasts of No Nation*, depicts a child soldier fighting in the civil war of an unnamed African country.

So far, the film, which has been seven years in the making, has no release date.

There also are rumours that Idris is to star in *Jurassic World*, the fourth film in the *Jurassic Park* series. But, while he is enjoying the excitement of many different projects coming together, he admits 2013 was an exceptionally big year for him with *Mandela: Long Walk to Freedom*, *Thor: The Dark World* and *Pacific Rim* all being released in quick succession: 'It's all out of sequence, by the time it comes out,' he said. 'This year looks incredibly busy for me because they're all coming out, at the same time. Really, the balance is being able to not over-saturate myself, in terms of all these films and stuff coming out at the same time.'

But characteristically Idris takes it all in his stride: 'I'm also continuing my career with stuff that may end up coming out later. *Mandela* was definitely a very, very challenging role for me, in the way that *Luther* is. It's very absorbing.

'Doing *Mandela* about a year ago now, and then doing *Luther*, they're both very complex characters that are demanding of my time. But this is what I do for a living. I enjoy the process of jumping from one person to another.'

Speaking just before he headed off to begin his next project, filming *The Gunman*, an action movie with *Taken* director Pierre Morel, which co-stars Sean Penn, Javier Bardem and Ray Winstone in Spain, he added: 'I have no base. I go from one job to another. I'm going to Barcelona next to do a film with Sean Penn.

'My part is quite small but instrumental. I took the job because of the cast,' he explains. 'It's amazing being around them. I've made a friend out of Sean, who has been incredibly generous and very supportive of my work. He's a big Stringer Bell fan and a big *Luther* fan and really wanted me to come and do this film because he wanted to work with me. He's a living legend and one of the best actors. He's a guy that hung out with Marlon Brando. I feel like I'm in great company.'

And Barcelona is conveniently located for his summer gig, another seven-week residency as the DJ for a nightclub in Ibiza, and his girlfriend and their baby are expected to travel with him. Although he feels rootless, back in his native Britain, he is not some semi-American hybrid but very much seen as one of us.

When Elba was selected to read the Edgar Albert Guest poem 'It Couldn't Be Done' for Team GB at the *BBC Sports Personality of the Year* in 2012, it was clear that he was becoming something of a national treasure. But to Idris that idea is hilarious: '*Me!* The way I live my life I'm two drinks from being in the tabloids every day,' he laughed. 'I'm no national treasure, I'm a fucking dutty rude boy! I consider myself an artist at this point. I am an artist; I have a few outlets for my art. I have my directing, my acting, film and my music and I want them to be varied and weird and different.

'I want people to go, "I don't know what he's going to do next". I love the idea of that. But I love to make music; I love it.'

And, even though he is an ambassador to The Prince's Trust, he is not expecting an OBE any time soon because he keeps lambasting the Royal Family in public. Recounting a recent US television interview with host Jimmy Kimmel, Idris said: 'I was saying about Prince Charles that he's smooth, you know, he's got the ring, the suit, the slick-back hair... he's a gangster! But, as soon as I said it, in my head I'm thinking, "Argh!"'

But he is proud of his royal connection and has a good relationship with the heir to the throne. Speaking about the Prince of Wales, Idris said: 'He's a good guy, I'm proud to be involved. I think when I turn up at these centres, kids relate to me as they know where I'm from. I know how it is for them. Usually they ask, "What's it like kissing Beyoncé, bruv?"'

And, although he is proud of his heritage, and Britain is proud of him, Idris still feels that he is living in 'no man's land': 'I don't have a place that I call home at the moment because there's no point,' he explained. 'I mean, I'm a travelling circus for a while. It's weird. Like, if I wanted to go home, there's nowhere to go – I just go to a hotel. But I've kind of gotten used to it. I am in between places, I can't really settle down yet.'

With his daughter in Atlanta, and his career based in Los Angeles, it is difficult for him to choose: 'I live in LA but I would consider moving my business to East London, my whole production side – the music, the movies set-up. It's a great place for inspiration as an artist.

'Growing older now, there's nothing you can tell me that I can't do. Why? Everything's about a skillset and I can learn those: step and process, digest it, practise.

'If I'm really honest, I'm too scared to look down. History maketh the man, but, if I thought about that journey, I could not do it. I wouldn't have the nuts if I planned it out. I'm not a brain surgeon, I'm an actor – I'm just telling stories, man, just telling stories.'

CHAPTER NINETEEN

BREAKING THROUGH CEILINGS

As 2016 dawned, Idris became sharply aware that he had made it. Finally he was where he always wanted to be. Memories of that ambitious East London lad, battling to be taken seriously in the fickle world of film, were starting to fade as it became clear that he had become firmly established as a bone fide A-list Hollywood superstar. As well as becoming a well-respected actor, he had also become a father again and the highest echelons of the British establishment were seeking his political opinions too.

This was to be the year that would see Mr. Elba summoned to give a speech in Parliament, scoop a clutch of prestigious awards, and even date a supermodel.

Everywhere he went Idris was trailed by a pack of hungry paparazzi but he refused to complain about all the attention, and almost every photo seemed to show him with a massive grin spread from ear to ear.

At the start of January, Idris admitted he was deeply honoured to be invited to deliver a keynote speech at the House of Commons on 'Diversity in the Media', a subject he had long felt deeply passionate about.

And he had impressed politicians hanging on to his every word as he revealed how 'good old Prince Charles' had given him his first break in the entertainment industry thanks to his grant from the Prince's Trust Charity.

But he also took the opportunity to warn that the lack of opportunity for black actors to land lead roles in the UK could result in yet more home grown talent leaving for America.

The star spoke at length in Parliament about the importance of creative industries to the British economy and called for 'imagination' and 'diversity of thought'. He also touched upon skin colour, gender, age, disability, sexual orientation and social background in a speech which he peppered with light hearted remarks that drew laughs from the packed committee room in Westminster, central London.

Speaking about his own path to stardom, Idris recalled: 'I finally got my first break in the creative industries from the Prince's Trust. Yes, good old Prince Charles came in there.'

Idris told how the grant helped him on his way into the theatre industry, and from there he moved into TV and film, explaining how his parents would never have been able to afford it otherwise: 'The Prince's Trust subsidised one of my first jobs with the National Music Youth Theatre' he said. 'They gave me £1,500, because my parents didn't have enough money. There were hardly any black kids, because none of us could afford it.

'And although back then I didn't get to meet Prince Charles, we had one thing in common. We both fell into the same line of work as our parents did.

'It's true. My dad worked in a car factory, so before I could get any work as an actor, I ended up doing night shifts at

Dagenham. In fact, Ford Dagenham had more opportunity and diversity than the TV industry I was trying to break into.'

Reminiscing over his humble upbringing in a Hackney high-rise tower block, Idris went on to highlight the fact that he used to fit tyres and now makes films in Hollywood. 'And the difference between those two lives is opportunity,' he said. 'By the way, I got my tyre-fitting job through the Youth Training Scheme.

'Before that, for a while I went to a disabled school because I had severe asthma.

'I'm a product of my imagination. Made in Hackney. Made in Newham. Made in Dagenham. But above all, I was made in my mind: I'm seeing it, thinking it, doing it.'

Idris made his much-publicised speech on the eve of a major TV industry conference on diversity, and took the opportunity to warn MPs that a lack of opportunities for black actors on British television is leaving talent 'on the scrapheap.' The actor hit out at the injustice of the situation, saying he had to move to America just so he could be considered for more leading roles in shows. He landed his breakthrough part of crime boss Stringer Bell in the series *The Wire*, as similar roles simply were not available to black actors in the UK.

Idris added that our television screens are at risk of not accurately reflecting society.

'The Britain I come from is the most successful, diverse, multicultural country on the earth,' he said. 'But here's my point: you wouldn't know it if you turned on the TV. So many of our creative decision-makers share the same background.

'People in the TV world often aren't the same as people in the real world. And there's an even bigger gap between people who make TV, and people who watch TV. I should know, I live in the TV world. And although there's a lot of reality TV, TV hasn't caught up with reality. Change is coming, but it's taking its sweet time,' he added.

Over one hundred Members of Parliament, including the culture minister Ed Vaizey, as well as senior television executives, attended his poignant speech at a meeting organised by Channel 4.

Idris went on to tell his audience that that he had to move to the US having seen a glass ceiling for black actors in Britain, and that if he had stayed he would have been side-lined to supporting parts, rather than having the chance to play leading roles.

'I was very close to hitting my forehead on it,' he said, adding that he would have been trapped playing "best friends" and "cop sidekick parts" and concluded he would have to go to the US if he wanted to be given starring roles in big dramas.

'But when you don't reflect the real world, too much talent gets trashed. Thrown on the scrapheap. Talent is everywhere, opportunity isn't. And talent can't reach opportunity.

'I knew I wasn't going to land a lead role. I knew there wasn't enough imagination in the industry for me to be seen as a lead. In other words, if I wanted to star in a British drama like *Luther* then I'd have to go to a country like America. And the other thing was, because I never saw myself on TV, I stopped watching TV. Instead I decided to just go out and become TV.'

His speech came as the entertainment industry on both sides of the Atlantic was under heavy scrutiny for the lack of diversity. Just days earlier, when the nominations were announced for the Academy Awards, there were no black actors or directors included on the Oscars shortlist. It provoked an outcry, with high profile stars condemning the largely white list of nominees.

Idris himself had been tipped to earn a nomination for best actor for his performance in *Beasts of No Nation*.

Actress Jada Pinkett Smith tweeted that 'people of color are always welcomed to give out awards . . . even entertain, but we are rarely recognized for our artistic accomplishments.'

Other British black actors have backed Idris in the past; speaking out publicly about the lack of opportunity, including *Homeland* star David Harewood.

He also suggested that he would not have landed the 'authoritative' role of intelligence agency head David Estes in the American political thriller if the show had been produced in the UK.

And Sophie Okonedo, who starred as Winnie Mandela in *Mrs Mandela*, and was nominated for an Oscar for her performance in *Hotel Rwanda*, had also previously said she that receives far more scripts from the US than she does from Britain: 'The balance is ridiculous,' she said. 'I'm still struggling in the UK in a way that my white counterparts at the same level wouldn't have quite the same struggle.

'People who started with me would have their own series by now, and I'm still fighting to get the second lead or whatever. I think I'm at a certain level and have a good range, so why isn't my inbox of English scripts busting at the seams in the same way as my American one is? There's something amiss there.'

And it was not just black actors who spoke out on the controversial issue – *Sherlock* star Benedict Cumberbatch also said he thought black British actors had a better chance of success in Hollywood than the UK: 'I think as far as coloured actors go it gets really difficult in the UK, and a lot of my friends have had more opportunities here [in the US] than in the UK and that's something that needs to change,' he explained on an American talk show. 'As long as we pay our taxes over here when we work, I think it's fair game. Meryl Streep can come over and play Margaret Thatcher.

'Why can't we come over and play in your sand pit?'

Fresh from his political triumph, Idris soon found himself being widely honoured for his acting skills too. He could not keep the smile off his face as he was named best actor at the *London Evening Standard* Film Awards, for his performance as Commandant in *Beasts of No Nation* - pipping his rival contenders Tom Courtenay and Michael Fassbender to the post.

At the star-studded ceremony held at Television Centre in West London, host Simon Amstell joked in his opening monologue that it was 'another great year for white men,' but when Idris picked up his prize from veteran actress Vanessa Redgrave he used his speech as an opportunity to address the on-going diversity row around the Oscar nominations.

Clutching the award for his performance as a ruthless rebel fighter in a West African civil war, he told how director Cary Fukunaga had worked for six years to secure enough funding to make the movie. The director, Idris explained, is half Japanese, half American, adding: 'The crew were from New York and Ghana, and the money came from all over. That is fucking diversity.'

Idris left a wet and windy London behind and jetted to Los Angeles for the start of the glitzy red carpet awards season. And he found himself among the top British winners at the SAG Awards, taking home not one but two awards at the ceremony. Confirming he was very much at the peak of his profession, Idris found himself seated among the biggest names at the top table for the event held at the famous Shrine Auditorium.

First Idris won the gong for Outstanding Performance by a Male Actor in a Television Movie or Miniseries for his leading role in the BBC drama *Luther*.

He also picked up the trophy for Outstanding Performance by a Male Actor in a Supporting Role in a Motion Picture for his work in the harrowing Netflix movie *Beasts of No Nation*, in which he portrayed an African warlord whose militia conscripts child soldiers.

'We made a film about real people and real lives and to be awarded for it is very special because a lot of people were damaged through that,' Idris said as he happily accepted his film award from actresses Brie Larson and Saoirse Ronan. 'Thank you for giving this film some light,' he added.

And when he jogged up to the stage for the second time in the same evening he said: 'Two wins in one night, that's incredible. I want to should out my beautiful children. When dad goes away, I think about you so much.'

He was joined by his teenage daughter Isan for the star-studded event, but just days later news emerged that he had split from his partner with whom he had a son, Winston, who was 22 months old.

Idris had become a father for the second time when his girlfriend make-up artist Naiyana Garth gave birth to their son in April 2014.

As the pregnancy news broke just weeks before the arrival, a source said at the time: 'Idris and Naiyana are so in love and this is the icing on the cake for them.

'They had been keeping it quiet as it's early in the pregnancy, but they've told family and friends and Naiyana is beginning to show.'

The couple were both said to 'feel lucky' to have found each other and were excited about meeting the new addition to their family.

The insider added: 'She is absolutely lovely and she's looking radiant. Her and Idris are a great couple.'

'Obviously Idris is a bit of a TV heart-throb so Naiyana is the envy of women across the country. But the truth is Idris is the one who really considers himself the lucky one. He's a great dad and she'll be a brilliant mum. They can't wait for their new arrival.'

Idris previously revealed how his eldest Isan remains entirely unimpressed with his career choice and the fame that comes with it.

He said: 'She's a nerd really, which I couldn't be more grateful for. She's not much impressed by what I do, but she does see how people react to me in the streets.

'She's very careful about it, wanting to steer me away from crowded streets and the like. I hate that she's losing some of her innocence, but I'm impressed by her level of awareness.'

When the new baby was born, Idris broke the news on Twitter, telling his more than 1 million followers about the new addition to the family. Idris chose his name in honour of his late father Winston, who died last September following a battle with lung cancer.

'My Son Winston Elba was born yesterday..Truly Amazing :-)' he captioned a shot of the infant gripping to his index finger.

Idris was later asked when he last felt truly happy, and replied: 'When my son Winston was born. And watching the magic that is childbirth. Of course I was there. Did I feel like a spare part? Nah, but I don't want to talk about it.'

Back in London to collect the Best Actor prize, again for his role in *Beasts of No Nation*, at the *NME* Awards Idris avoided answering a flurry of questions about his family.

After almost two years of being a devoted partner and father he had quietly moved into a rented flat close to his ex and their infant son.

Meanwhile American rapper K Michelle told a television

show that she had a romance with Idris. She explained: 'When I met him I did find out he had a woman. But I did not know they still had that situation. So I kind of looked up and saw that I was the side chick.' Idris did not comment on these reports at the time.

Of course, female attention was not new for Idris, who has past form for not partaking in conventional family life.

As a young man working as a DJ on a pirate radio station he was known as Mr Kipling, after someone said, 'Idris, you've got more tarts than Mr Kipling.'

He split from his first wife, make-up artist Henne Norgaard, while she was pregnant with their daughter, Isan, soon after landing his breakthrough role on *The Wire*.

His second marriage lasted only a day — four years after his first marriage collapsed, after a party in 2006, he married a lawyer called Sonya Hamlin in Las Vegas, only to file for an annulment a day later.

And then, while visiting his daughter Isan in Atlanta, where she was then living, he met a pole dancer named Desiree Newberry at the strip club Magic Sky. They started living together in a beach house in Miami, Florida, and when she gave birth to a son, named Otenga, in 2010, Idris was thrilled.

But after becoming suspicious that the child was not his because he looked nothing like him, and took a paternity test. The results were unequivocal. He was not Otenga's father.

That betrayal has haunted him ever since, and he has subsequently said: 'I wasn't knocked out. I stood right back up, and I ain't aiming to take another punch in the face ever again'.

By 2013, though, he had met Naiyana, another make-up artist, who had previously worked with chef Jamie Oliver and actors Rupert Everett and Freddie Fox.

Within a year she was expecting their child and accompanied him, with her large pregnancy bump proudly on display, on the red carpet to the Golden Globes and Oscars in early 2014, where he was nominated for his portrayal of Nelson Mandela in *Mandela: Long Walk To Freedom*.

Baby Winston was born in April 2014, and should have heralded the happy-ever-after that had so far eluded Idris.

But, as it later emerged, that rumoured relationship with rap artist K Michelle, whose real name is Kimberly Michelle Pate, had developed. They met in the spring of 2014 when he directed a music video for her.

She was immediately smitten, soon after meeting Idris she gushed: 'It's really crazy to see how humble and down to earth this man is. He's so creative. He's so in the zone.' A few months later, she went on a chat show in America and said 'We just clicked,' before going on to say how the romance was her inspiration for her album *Anybody Wanna Buy A Heart*.

And the lyrics of her hit single 'Maybe I Should Call' seemed to reveal a little more about the nature of their relationship: 'Long distance in the way of what could be / even when you're here, you're not with me / she's having the child I should've carried / I'll be damned if y'all get married.'

She went on to tell an interviewer: 'There was a situation. He has a child and I'm not going to get in the way of that.

'Y'all not gonna call me the home wrecker. Me, I desire a lot of attention and time and when there's a newborn, you have to give your time and attention to them.'

Her outspoken remarks also went some way to explain why Naiyana failed to accompany Idris to the Golden Globes in early 2016. Idris told reporters that Naiyana was unable to travel with the baby and took his daughter Isan instead. But it later emerged via social media that Naiyana was on a beach in South-East Asia with baby Winston at the time.

Naiyana was absent again at the Screen Actors Guild Awards in Los Angeles, and nor was she by his side when he appeared at the *Evening Standard* Film Awards in London. She also failed to get a mention in either of his acceptance speeches.

And just a few days later, the actor was seen emerging from a New York nightclub with longtime friend and supermodel Naomi Campbell, although neither Naiyana nor agents for Idris would comment on whether their relationship was over.

Naomi was rumoured to be in America for hip replacement surgery at the age of 45. The stunning supermodel and star of TV hit *Empire*, who has been walking the world's catwalks for three decades, was seen using a cane with claims she had been discussing her hip surgery plans at the time. Idris and Naomi have been friends for years and often support each other at their respective acting and fashion events.

Idris joined a star-studded line up at Naomi's 'Fashion For Relief' charity fundraiser, arriving at London's Westfield shopping centre alongside chart-topper Tinie Tempah to support Naomi's bid to raise money for Ebola in 2014. And Naomi took to her Twitter account to publicly congratulate him on his SAG Awards win, in the midst of the Oscars' race row.

Naomi tweeted him just last week after his SAG awards win, and said: 'Congratulations @Idriselba you deserve your double WIN. @SAGawards'

At the same time as his eventful love life, Idris continued to ride high professionally. Fans were delighted when he agreed to film two special episodes of *Luther* for BBC television to air over the Christmas of 2015. He had previously hinted that he was done with the show that made him a household name.

But he was unable to resist one last chance to play the angry London detective John Luther, a cop who seems not to care what anyone else thinks, haunted by the brutal murder of his wife Zoe, played by Indira Varma in series one.

'I think Luther would always be the kind of person who chases people if they're doing wrong,' said Idris when the show returned amid a fanfare of anticipation. 'He can't help himself.'

First made in 2010, the show was a hit around the world including, significantly, on BBC America where some of the world's best directors suddenly paid attention to Idris.

With leading roles finally on the table, including *Mandela* and Ridley Scott's *Prometheus* and *Pacific Rim*, Idris was understandably reluctant to commit to a fourth series: 'When we finished it last time I was fed up with it,' he admitted. 'I'm not sure whether I wanted it to be the end but that version of *Luther* had to stop. I would still like there to be a *Luther* film but for both me and the writer Neil Cross this feels like the pilot of a film.

'This is Luther on his next chapter; he's slightly older and a bit smarter and wiser. It's good to be back. We have an audience that's very loyal and demanding and I hope they feel satisfied that we're back even though we've been off the air for over two years.

'I don't think either of us – Neil or me – were completely satisfied with the ending of the last one. It felt like there were some unanswered questions. Perhaps we answer them here but as we close down one chapter we open a new one; we keep the story growing.'

The new episodes started soon after the last ended - Luther was still devastated by the death of his partner DS Justin Ripley, the only man who always believed in him, at the hands of a vigilante killer.

He had taken leave from the Metropolitan Police and was licking his wounds in solitude, living in a rundown house on a remote cliff top. His battered old Volvo car lay unused and the familiar overcoat had been replaced with a parka. But his peace was shattered when a former colleague turns up with news of Luther's murderous nemesis Alice Morgan – played by Ruth Wilson, who recently starred alongside Idris' former *The Wire* co-star Dominic West in *The Affair*.

The only murderer Luther failed to jail, Alice was the sexy but psychopathic genius who he knew was evil but had talked about running away with.

With a new serial killer is on the loose in London, Luther was lured back to work in the capital.

Neil Cross revealed that Idris had not been his first choice to play Luther but over the years, as both have taken producing roles on the show, they have become extremely close friends.

Neil, who also wrote *Spooks*, explained that he actually took stories from Idris' own life as inspiration for Luther scripts and the actor himself even admitted that sometimes he found it hard to know where Luther starts and Idris ends.

'I tend to try and do Luther when I'm most tired; I throw all my pent-up emotions into the character and Neil instinctively knows that,' said Idris.

'There's a lot of emotion I have to dig into to get Luther and the way Neil writes is by asking me questions about my life. When I first played Luther I had to imagine what his angst was but now I know him, I understand his angst. It's not too dissimilar to mine. Pent-up emotions, big heart, over-ambitious. Neil's aware of my life and that comes into my character a little bit.

'Ultimately John's a workaholic; I'm a workaholic too. I throw everything into what I do, period. John does the same.

He's a civil servant and I'm an actor but John over-extends himself emotionally and I do that.

'I get closer to the truth of John Luther via my own experiences and that's a very special relationship that you can have when you're in a long-running series. This one is bigger and better and we've upped the ante. I'm happy it's back.'

Idris credits Luther as the show that really showed the world what he was capable of, and as a result he is still doing brilliantly today.

His Netflix movie *Beasts of No Nation* received lots of Oscar buzz and he recently finished filming the new *Star Trek* movie as well as providing voices for *Finding Nemo* follow-up *Finding Dory* and as Shere Khan in the live-action remake of *The Jungle Book*.

Idris also finds time to continue his successful side-line as a superstar DJ – opening for Madonna at her Berlin concert in 2015 – and has co-designed a fashion range for Superdry clothing which the British brand hopes will open the American market for them.

And, of course, there is a smart bet to be made on him being given the role as the next James Bond. He's one of the bookies' favourites but there's been a lot of debate over whether the world is ready for a black Bond, with author Anthony Horowitz, author of the latest Bond novel *Trigger Mortis*, questioning whether Idris is 'too street' for the role. His remarks were interpreted as a racial slur, which he was quick to deny, adding: 'Idris Elba is a terrific actor, but I can think of other black actors who would do it better. For me, Idris Elba is a bit too rough to play the part. It's not a colour issue. I think he probably is a bit too 'street' for Bond. Is it a question of being suave? Yeah.'

Former Bond star Pierce Brosnan also waded into the row,

throwing shade onto Idris' hopes of filling the coveted role, by saying: 'He'll be male and he'll be white.

'A female James Bond, no, I think it has to be male. James Bond is a guy, he's all male. His name is James, his name is James Bond,' Brosnan insisted when asked who might be next in line to play Ian Fleming's famous spy.

Although hunky leading men including Damien Lewis, Tom Hardy, James Norton, Tom Hiddlestone and Aidan Turner were also being touted as possible replacements, Daniel Craig has not at the time of writing confirmed whether he wants to give up the job after four films so the controversy is – for the time being at least – academic.

Although Idris himself has admitted he is humbled by fans supporting the idea, he is clearly sick to death of being asked about it. 'I just don't want to be the black James Bond,' he said. 'Sean Connery wasn't the Scottish James Bond and Daniel Craig wasn't the blue-eyed James Bond so if I played him I don't want to be called the black James Bond.'

Idris has said that he feels like a Bond star, despite never having actually played 007, and he's had enough: 'It feels like I'm campaigning and I'm not,' he explained. 'At first it was harmless – oh I know, wouldn't it be great? And now it's started off racial debates.

'I'm probably the most famous Bond actor in the world, and I've not even played the role. Enough is enough. I can't talk about it anymore.'

While he has long been a popular choice among fans to take over the role of James Bond, his latest film *Bastille Day* might provide the best indication yet of whether he should inherit 007's license to kill.

The first international trailer for *Bastille Day* featured Idris *and Game of Thrones* actor Richard Madden teaming up to stop an explosive terrorist attack in France. With plenty of tension, fast-paced action, and more than a few close-ups of Idris shooting first and asking questions later (and showing exactly the sort of certainty of purpose that's a necessary quality in a James Bond), the preview could serve double duty as a compelling action-thriller and a feature-length audition for Idris.

In the film, he plays a tough CIA agent who goes rogue after uncovering a dangerous conspiracy linked to a potential terrorist attack in France. He is forced to team up with an American pickpocket played by Madden in order to investigate the case, and the pair soon find themselves targeted by enemies who might be rooted within the government itself.

But whether or not he is crowned as the next Bond, Idris has a golden future ahead as both an actor and a political activist – albeit a rather reluctant one. He now finds himself heralded as a black man who has broken through glass ceilings.

But he's never enjoyed being a role model and he sighs whenever it is mentioned: 'Things are changing, there's a lot of work to do but it's definitely moving in the right direction,' he says.

'People are more aware of the problems that are being faced but it's one of those problems that won't be fixed overnight.'

FILMOGRAPHY

Star Trek Beyond (2016)
Directed by Justin Lin
Screenplay by Simon Pegg
Released by Paramount Pictures
Cast: Chris Pine, Simon Pegg

Finding Dory (2016)
Directed by Andrew Stanton
Screenplay by Andrew Stanton
Released by Walt Disney Studios Motion Pictures
Cast: Ellen DeGeneres, Albert Brooks

The Jungle Book (2016)
Directed by Jon Favreau
Screenplay by Justin Marks
Released by Walt Disney Studios Motion Pictures
Cast: Bill Murray, Ben Kingsley

Zootopia (2016)
Directed by Bryon Howard and Rich Moore
Screenplay by Jared Bush, Phil Johnston
Released by Walt Disney Studios
Cast: Ginnifer Goodwin, Jason Bateman

Beasts of No Nation (2015)
Directed by Cary Fukunaga
Screenplay by Cary Fukunaga
Released by Netflix
Cast: Kurt Egyiawan, Jude Akuwudike

Avengers: Age of Ultron (2015)
Directed by Joss Whedon
Screenplay by Joss Whedon
Released by Walt Disney Studios Motion Pictures
Cast: Robert Downey Jr., Chris Evans

Second Coming (2014) as Mark
Directed by Debbie Tucker Green
Screenplay by Debbie Tucker Green
Released by British Film Institute
Cast: Nicola Walker, Lee Nicholas Harris

The Gunman (2014) as Dupont
Directed by Pierre Morel
Screenplay by Don MacPherson
Released by StudioCanal
Cast: Sean Penn, Javier Bardem

No Good Deed (2014) as Colin
Directed by Sam Miller

Screenplay by Aimee Lagos
Released by Screen Gems
Cast: Taraji P. Henson, Leslie Bibb

Thor: The Dark World (2013) as Heimdall
Directed by Alan Taylor
Screenplay by Christopher Yost
Released by Marvel Entertainment
Cast: Chris Hemsworth, Natalie Portman,
Anthony Hopkins

Mandela: Long Walk to Freedom (2013) as
   Nelson Mandela
Directed by Justin Chadwick
Screenplay by William Nicholson
Released by Videovision Entertainment
Cast: Naomie Harris, Tony Kgoroge

Pacific Rim (2013) as Stacker Pentecost
Directed by Guillermo del Toro
Screenplay by Travis Beacham
Released by Warner Bros
Cast: Charlie Hunnam, Diego Klattenhoff

Prometheus (2012) as Janek
Directed by Ridley Scott
Screenplay by Jon Spaihts
Released by Twentieth Century Fox
Cast: Noomi Rapace, Michael Fassbender,
   Charlize Theron

Ghost Rider: Spirit of Vengeance (2011) as Moreau
Directed by Mark Neveldine
Screenplay by Scott M. Gimple
Released by Columbia Pictures
Cast: Nicolas Cage, Violante Placido

Thor (2011) as Heimdall
Directed by Kenneth Branagh
Screenplay by Ashley Miller
Released by Paramount Pictures
Cast: Chris Hemsworth, Natalie Portman,
  Anthony Hopkins

Takers (2010) as Gordon Jennings
Directed by John Luessenhop
Screenplay by Peter Allen
Released by Screen Gems
Cast: Chris Brown, Hayden Christensen

The Losers (2010) as Roque
Directed by Sylvain White
Screenplay by Peter Berg
Released by Warner Bros
Cast: Zoe Saldana, Chris Evans

Legacy: Black Ops (2010) as Malcolm Gray
Directed by Thomas Ikimi
Screenplay Thomas Ikimi
Released by Black Camel Pictures
Cast: William Hope, Richard Brake

Obsessed (2009) as Derek
Directed by Steve Shill
Screenplay by David Loughery
Released by Screen Gems
Cast: Beyoncé, Ali Larter

The Unborn (2009) as Arthur Wyndham
Directed by David S. Goyer
Screenplay by David S. Goyer
Released by Rogue Pictures
Cast: Gary Oldman, Odette Annable

The Human Contract (2008) as Larry
Directed by Jada Pinkett Smith
Screenplay by Jada Pinkett Smith
Released by Overbrook Entertainment
Cast: Jason Clarke, Paz Vega

RocknRolla (2008) as Mumbles
Directed by Guy Ritchie
Screenplay by Guy Ritchie
Released by Warner Bros
Cast: Gerard Butler, Tom Wilkinson, Thandie Newton

Prom Night (2008) as Detective Winn
Directed by Nelson McCormick
Screenplay by J.S. Cardone
Released by Alliance Films
Cast: Brittany Snow, Scott Porter

This Christmas (2007) as Quentin Whitfield
Directed by Preston A. Whitmore II
Screenplay by Preston A. Whitmore II
Released by Facilitator Films
Cast: Delroy Lindo, Loretta Devine

American Gangster (2007) as Tango
Directed by Ridley Scott
Screenplay by Steven Zallian
Released by Universal
Cast: Denzel Washington, Russell Crowe

28 Weeks Later (2007) as Stone
Directed by Juan Carlos Fresnadillo
Screenplay by Rowan Joffe
Released by 20th Century Fox
Cast: Robert Carlyle, Rose Byrne

The Reaping (2007) as Ben
Directed by Stephen Hopkins
Screenplay by Carey Hayes
Released by Warner Bros
Cast: Hilary Swank, David Morrissey

Daddy's Little Girls (2007) as Monty
Directed by Tyler Perry
Screenplay by Tyler Perry
Released by Lionsgate Films
Cast: Gabrielle Union, Louis Gossett Jnr

FILMOGRAPHY

The Gospel (2005) as Reverend Charles Frank
Directed by Rob Hardy
Screenplay by Rob Hardy
Released by Rainforest Films
Cast: Boris Kodjoe, Nona Gaye

One Love (2003) as Aaron
Directed by Rick Elgood
Screenplay by Trevor D. Rhone
Released by One Love Films
Cast: Leon C. Allen, Cherine Anderson

Buffalo Soldier (2001) as Kimborough
Directed by Gregor Jordan
Screenplay by Robert O'Connor
Released by Odeon Film
Cast: Joaquin Phoenix, Anna Paquin

Sorted (2000) as Jam
Directed by Alexander Jovy
Screenplay by Alexander Jovy
Released by Excell Film Agentur
Cast: Matthew Rhys, Sienna Guillory

Belle Maman (1999) as Grégoire
Directed by Gabriel Aghion
Screenplay by Gabriel Aghion
Released by Arena Films
Cast: Catherine Deneuve

TELEVISION

Luther (2010 – 2015, four series) as DCI John Luther
Idris Elba's How Clubbing Changed the World as himself
Idris Elba: King of Speed as himself
Idris Elba: No Limits as himself
Aqua Teen Hunger Force (2011, one episode) as Police Officer
Luther (2010–2013, three series) as DCI John Luther
The Big C (2010, four episodes) as Lenny
The Office (2009, seven episodes) as Charles Miner
The No. 1 Ladies' Detective Agency (2008, one series) as
  Charlie Gotso
Queens Supreme (2007, one series) as Carla
All in the Game (2006, TV Movie) as Paul
Jonny Zero (2005, one episode) as Hodge
Sometimes in April (2005, TV Movie) as Augustin
Girlfriends (2005, one episode) as Paul Raymond
The Wire (2002–2004, three series) as Russell 'Stringer' Bell
CSI: Miami (2003, one episode) as Angelo Sedaris
Soul Food (2003, one episode) as Smitty
Hack (2002, one episode) as Mac Boone
The Inspector Lynley Mysteries (2002, one episode) as
  Robert Gabriel
Law & Order (2001, one episode) as Lonnie Liston
London's Burning (2001, two episodes) as Lance Corporal
  Frost
In Defence (2000, one episode) as PC Paul Fraser
Dangerfield (1999, twelve episodes) as Matt Gregory
Ultraviolet (1998, six episodes) as Vaughan Rice
Verdict (1998, one episode) as PC Brian Rawlinson
Family Affairs (1997, five episodes) as Tim Webster
Insiders (1997, six episodes) as Robinson Bennett

FILMOGRAPHY

Silent Witness (1997, two episodes) as Charlie
Crocodile Shoes II (1996, one episode) as Jo-Jo
Crucial Tales (1996, one episode) as Benton
The Governor (1996, two episodes) as Officer Chiswick
Ruth Rendell Mysteries (1996, four episodes) as Raffy
The Bill (1995, two episodes) as Earl Lee and Alex Mason
Bramwell (1995, one episode) as Charlie Carter
Absolutely Fabulous (1995, one episode) as Hilton
Space Precinct (1994, one episode) as Pizza Delivery Man
2point4 Children (1994, one episode) as Parachute Instructor

PRODUCER

No Good Deed (2014) Executive Producer
Idris Elba's How Clubbing Changed the World (2014, TV documentary) Executive Producer
Luther (2010–2013, TV series) Associate Producer
Walk Like a Panther (2011, one episode) Executive Producer, 1 episode
Demons Never Die (2011) Executive Producer
Milk & Honey (2011, TV Series) Executive Producer
How Hip Hop Changed the World (2011, documentary) Executive Producer
Legacy: Black Ops (2010) Executive Producer

DIRECTOR

Playhouse Presents (2013, one episode)
The Pavement Psychologist (2013)